Teacher's Manual

ACADEMIC
Listening
ENCOUNTERS

LIFE IN SOCIETY

Listening

Note Taking

Discussion

Kim Sanabria

Intermediate to High Intermediate

CAMBRIDGE
UNIVERSITY PRESS

PUBLISHED BY THE PRESS SYNDICATE OF THE UNIVERSITY OF CAMBRIDGE
The Pitt Building, Trumpington Street, Cambridge, United Kingdom

CAMBRIDGE UNIVERSITY PRESS
The Edinburgh Building, Cambridge CB2 2RU, UK
40 West 20th Street, New York, NY 10011-4211, USA
477 Williamstown Road, Port Melbourne, VIC 3207, Australia
Ruiz de Alarcón 13, 28014 Madrid, Spain
Dock House, The Waterfront, Cape Town 8001, South Africa

http://www.cambridge.org

First published 2004

Printed in the United States of America
Typeset in New Aster and Frutiger

Book design: Adventure House, NYC
Layout services: Page Designs International

ACADEMIC ENCOUNTERS

The *Academic Encounters* series uses authentic materials and a sustained content approach to teach students the academic skills they need to take college courses in English. There are two books in the series for each content focus: an *Academic Encounters* title and an *Academic Listening Encounters* title. As the series continues to grow, books at different levels and with different content area concentrations will be added. Please consult your catalog or contact your local sales representative for a current list of available titles.

Titles in the *Academic Encounters* series at publication:

Content Focus and Level	Components	Academic Encounters	Academic Listening Encounters
HUMAN BEHAVIOR High Intermediate to Low Advanced	Student's Book Teacher's Manual Class Audio Cassettes Class Audio CDs	ISBN 0 521 47658 5 ISBN 0 521 47660 7	ISBN 0 521 60620 9 ISBN 0 521 57820 5 ISBN 0 521 57819 1 ISBN 0 521 78357 7
LIFE IN SOCIETY Intermediate to High Intermediate	Student's Book Teacher's Manual Class Audio Cassettes Class Audio CDs	ISBN 0 521 66616 3 ISBN 0 521 66613 9	ISBN 0 521 75483 6 ISBN 0 521 75484 4 ISBN 0 521 75485 2 ISBN 0 521 75486 0

Contents

Introduction

This introduction provides a description of the *Academic Encounters* series and an overview of the *Academic Listening Encounters* books. It also includes general teaching suggestions and guidelines for classroom use. The next section contains specific chapter-by-chapter teaching suggestions for *Academic Listening Encounters: Life in Society*. Answers corresponding to its tasks are also found in the second section. Additional activities are suggested at the end of each unit. The third section of this Teacher's Manual contains the complete Listening Script of the material on the audio program for *Academic Listening Encounters: Life in Society*. Photocopiable quizzes on the lectures, with answers, are provided in the fourth section.

ABOUT THE *ACADEMIC ENCOUNTERS* SERIES

This content-based series is for non-native speakers of English preparing to study in English at the community college or university level, but it is also suitable for native speakers of English who need to improve their academic skills for further study. The series consists of *Academic Encounters* books that help students improve their reading, study skills, and writing; and *Academic Listening Encounters* books that concentrate on listening, note-taking, and discussion skills. Each reading book corresponds in theme to a listening book, and each pair of theme-linked books focuses on an academic subject commonly taught in North American universities and community colleges. For example, *Academic Encounters: Life in Society* and *Academic Listening Encounters: Life in Society* both focus on sociology; likewise, *Academic Encounters: Human Behavior* and *Academic Listening Encounters: Human Behavior* both focus on psychology and human communications. A reading book and a listening book with the same content focus may be used together to teach a complete four-skills course in English for Academic Purposes.

ABOUT *ACADEMIC LISTENING ENCOUNTERS: LIFE IN SOCIETY*

Academic Listening Encounters: Life in Society is a content-based listening, note-taking, and discussion text. It focuses on topics covered in sociology courses offered in North American community colleges and universities. The student who will benefit most from this course will be at the intermediate to high-intermediate level. The topics included have been chosen for their universal appeal, but as students progress through the book, they will also acquire a basic foundation in the concepts and vocabulary of sociology. The listening, note-taking, and discussion tasks that students work through are designed to help them develop the skills they need for study in any academic discipline.

ACADEMIC LISTENING ENCOUNTERS
LISTENING, NOTE-TAKING, AND DISCUSSION BOOKS

The approach

Focusing on a particular academic discipline allows students to gain a sustained experience with one field and encounter concepts and terminology that overlap and grow more complex. It provides students with a realistic sense of studying a course in college. As language and concepts recur and as their skills develop, students begin to gain confidence until ultimately, they feel that they have enough background in the content focus area to actually take a course in that subject in order to fulfill part of their general education requirements.

The format

Each listening, note-taking, and discussion book consists of five units on different aspects of the discipline. Units are divided into two chapters. Each chapter has four sections and includes an introductory listening exercise, a selection of informal interviews, an opportunity for students to conduct and present a topic-related project, and a two-part academic lecture. A variety of listening, note-taking, and discussion tasks accompany the listening material. Chapters are structured to maximize students' comprehension of the chapter topic. Vocabulary and ideas are recycled through the four sections of each chapter and recur in later chapters, as students move from listening to discussion, and from informal to academic discourse.

A chapter-by-chapter Plan of the Book appears in the front of the Student's Book and an alphabetized Task Index is at the back of the Student's Book.

The audio program

The center of *Academic Listening Encounters: Life in Society* is its authentic listening material. The audio program for each chapter includes a warm-up listening exercise designed to introduce the topic, informal interviews that explore a particular aspect of the chapter topic, and a two-part academic lecture on another aspect of the topic. Each of these three types of listening experience exposes students to a different style of discourse, while recycling vocabulary and concepts.

Tasks that are designed to practice a listening skill and involve listening to the audio material (for example, *Listening for Specific Information, Listening for Opinions,* or *Note Taking: Listening for Organizational Phrases*), have an earphones icon 🎧 next to the title. This symbol indicates that there is material in the audio program related to the task. A second symbol ▶ PLAY indicates the exact point within the task when the audio material should be played.

The complete audio program, which contains the recorded material for the listening and note-taking tasks, is available on both audio CDs and audio cassettes. The listening script of the complete audio program is in the third section of this Teacher's Manual; it may also be found at the

Academic Encounters section of the Cambridge website, *www.cambridge.org/esl*. An audio CD of the academic lectures, which are an important part of the audio program, is included in the back of each Student's Book to provide students with additional listening practice.

The skills

The three main skills developed in *Academic Listening Encounters* books are listening, note taking, and discussion. Listening is a critical area because unlike text on a page, spoken words are difficult to review. In addition to the content and vocabulary of what they hear, students are challenged by different accents, speeds of delivery, and other features of oral discourse. Tasks in the *Academic Listening Encounters* books guide students in techniques for improving their listening comprehension. These tasks also develop note-taking skills in a structured format that teaches students to write down what they hear in ways that will make it easier to retrieve the information. After the listening and note-taking practice comes an invitation to discussion. Students discuss what they have heard, voice their opinions, compare their experiences, and articulate and exchange viewpoints with other class members, thus making the material their own. Additionally, each chapter gives students the opportunity to work on a project related to the topic, such as conducting a survey or undertaking research, and teaches them the skills necessary to present their findings.

Task commentary boxes

Whenever a task type occurs for the first time in the book, it is headed by a colored commentary box that explains what skill is being practiced and why it is important. When the task occurs again later in the book, it may be accompanied by another commentary box, either as a reminder or to present new information about the skill. At the back of the book, there is an alphabetized index of all the tasks. Page references in boldface indicate tasks that are headed by commentary boxes.

Opportunities for student interaction

Many of the tasks in *Academic Listening Encounters* are divided into steps. Some of these steps are to be done by the student working alone, others by students in pairs or in small groups, and still others by the teacher with the whole class. To make the book as lively as possible, student interaction has been built into most activities. Thus, although the books focus on listening and note-taking skills, discussion is fundamental to each chapter. Students often work collaboratively and frequently compare answers in pairs or small groups.

Order of units

The units do not have to be taught in the order in which they appear in the book, although this order is recommended. To a certain extent, tasks do increase in complexity so that, for example, a note-taking task later in the book may draw upon information that has been included in an earlier unit. Teachers who want to use the material out of order may, however, consult the Plan of the Book at the front of the book or the Task Index at the back of the book to see what information has been presented in earlier units.

Course length

Each chapter of a listening, note-taking, and discussion book is divided into four sections and represents approximately 7–11 hours of classroom material. Thus, with a 90-minute daily class, a teacher could complete all ten chapters in a ten-week course. For use with a shorter course, a teacher could omit chapters or activities within chapters. The material could also be expanded with the use of guest speakers, debates, movies, and other authentic recorded material (see "Additional Ideas" at the end of each unit in this manual).

CHAPTER FORMAT

1 Getting Started (approximately 1 hour of class time)

This section contains a short reading task and a listening task. The reading is designed to activate students' prior knowledge about the topic, provide them with general concepts and vocabulary, and stimulate their interest. Comprehension and discussion questions elicit their engagement in the topic.

The listening task in this section is determined by the chapter content and involves one of a variety of responses. The task may require students to complete a chart, do a matching exercise, or listen for specific information. The task provides skill-building practice and also gives students listening warm-up on the chapter topic.

2 American Voices (approximately 2–3½ hours of class time)

This section contains informal recorded interviews on issues related to the chapter. It is divided into three subsections:

Before the Interviews (approximately ½ hour)

This subsection contains a pre-listening task that calls on students to predict the content of the interview or share what they already know about the topic from their personal experience. Take enough time with this task for all students to contribute. The more they invest in the topic at this point, the more they will get out of the interviews.

Interviews (approximately 1–2 hours)

In this subsection, students listen to interviews related to the topic of the chapter. In most chapters the interviewees are native speakers of English, but voices of immigrants to the United States also enrich the discussions. The interviewees are of different ages and ethnic and social backgrounds, allowing students to gain exposure to the rich and diverse reality of speakers of English. The interviews are divided into two parts to facilitate comprehension: each part can include from one to three interviewees.

Each interview segment begins with a boxed vocabulary preview that glosses words and phrases students may not know. The vocabulary is given in the context in which students will hear it. Reading this vocabulary aloud and exploring its meaning within the context will facilitate students' comprehension.

After each vocabulary preview, students are given the opportunity to scan the upcoming task. Then they listen to the interview and go on to complete the particular task, which might include listening for main ideas or details, drawing inferences, or taking notes on the material in order to retell what they have heard. This approach provides a framework for listening, teaches basic listening skills, and allows students to demonstrate their understanding of the interviews,

After the Interviews (approximately ½–1 hour)
In this subsection, students explore the topic more deeply through examining graphic material related to the content of the interviews, thinking critically about what they have heard, or sharing their perspective. Most of the tasks in this section are for pairs or small groups and allow for informal feedback from every student.

3 In Your Own Voice (approximately 1½–2½ hours)

This section continues to build on the chapter topic and is designed to give students the opportunity to take creative control of the topic at hand. Specific tasks are determined by the chapter content. They may include

- *Personalizing the content,* in which students talk with partners or in small groups, sharing their experiences and supporting their points of view,
- *Gathering data,* in which students conduct surveys or interviews of classmates or people outside the class, or in which they undertake small research projects,
- *Presenting data,* in which students organize their data and present it individually or in small groups,
- *Responding to presentations,* in which students discuss the content of presentations and analyze the effectiveness of a presenter's style.

4 Academic Listening and Note Taking (approximately 2½–4 hours)

This section contains a formal, recorded, academic lecture related to the topic of the chapter. It is divided into three subsections:

Before the Lecture (1–1½ hours)
The first task of this subsection asks students to predict the content of the lecture, explore what they already know about the topic, or build their background knowledge and vocabulary by doing a task related to a brief reading, syllabus, or other written entry. As with *Before the Interview,* this section promotes the student's investment in the topic.

Each chapter then proceeds to an academic note-taking skill, determined by the language of the lecture itself and sequenced to build upon skills studied in previous chapters. The skill is explained in a task commentary box, and the listening task is designed to practice it. The recorded material used for the task is drawn from the lecture.

Lecture (1–1½ hours)

In this subsection, students hear the lecture itself. To facilitate comprehension, all lectures are divided into two parts.

Each lecture part begins with a matching or multiple-choice vocabulary task to prepare students for the language they will encounter in the lecture and help them develop their ability to guess meaning from context. Potentially unfamiliar words and phrases are given in the context in which they will be used in the lecture. Reading the items aloud, studying their pronunciation, and exploring their use and meaning will prepare students for hearing them in the lecture.

Following the vocabulary task, students preview a comprehension task designed to provide a framework for their listening and note taking. The task may involve completing a summary or outline, or answering comprehension questions. The task may recycle the note-taking skill taught before the lecture, or add a related skill. Students are instructed to take notes during each part of the lecture, and then use their notes to complete the lecture comprehension task. Previewing the task will enable students to answer the questions in a more confident and focused manner.

After the Lecture (½–1 hour)

This subsection invites students to share their perspective through discussion questions that allow them to analyze the chapter content more critically. It may also present additional information or ask students to apply what they have learned.

GENERAL TEACHING SUGGESTIONS

Section Introductions

Each chapter in the Student's Book is divided into four sections. Each section begins with a brief preview: *In this section you will . . . .* Always read these previews together with the class and answer any questions that arise. Take enough time with this task for all students to contribute.

Tasks and Commentary Boxes

Virtually every activity throughout *Academic Listening Encounters* is presented as a task. Each task practices a specific language or thinking skill critical for academic-bound students of English. Most tasks are recycled throughout the book. (See the Plan of the Book in the front of the Student's Book or the Task Index at the back of the Student's Book.) The first time a task title appears, it is followed by a shaded task commentary box containing information about the task. Always read this commentary and check for understanding. Ask students: *What are we doing in this exercise? Why is this useful?*

Listening Tasks

Before students listen to the recorded material and complete the task, make sure that they read over the task and think about what information they will need to listen for.

Replay audio excerpts as many times as you think will benefit the majority of students and enable them to complete tasks successfully, including the interviews and lectures. Students are not expected to catch every word; it is not necessary.

As an alternative to the recording, you may try reading the lectures to your students. (See the section titled Listening Script in this Teacher's Manual.) Try to incorporate appropriate stress, intonation, and body language.

In Your Own Voice

In Your Own Voice (Section 3) usually concludes with students giving oral presentations about a project they have completed. Keep students on task by having them respond to the presentations. They can take notes, ask questions, make comments, and suggest possible ways presenters could improve their style. You may also want to give a content quiz on the presentations. One way to do this is to use your own notes to write one general question about each presentation. Then dictate your questions and allow students to refer to their notes in order to respond.

Photos, Cartoons, and Drawings

All of the art in the Student's Book is intended to build interest and comprehension. In many cases, students are directed to think about the art as part of a task. In cases where they are not specifically asked to do this – such as the art at the beginning of units and chapters – be sure to draw their attention to the art and discuss its connection to the topic.

Vocabulary

Unfamiliar vocabulary is a great stumbling block to comprehension, so a great effort has been made to gloss or preteach most of the language that is unfamiliar to students. In each part of Section 2 (American Voices), have students read the vocabulary and glosses in the box by themselves first; then read the vocabulary items aloud so that students can hear how the words are pronounced. Check for understanding of glosses given in the vocabulary boxes.

Each part of the lecture in Section 4 (Academic Listening and Note Taking) begins with a task called "Guessing vocabulary from context." Begin by reading the vocabulary aloud. When checking the vocabulary task, give the correct answers yourself only as a last resort.

Any photos or realia that you can bring to class will help with comprehension and retention of vocabulary.

Comprehension and Discussion Questions

One of the goals of *Academic Listening Encounters* is to develop oral fluency, and for this reason there is a great deal of pair and small group work. If students have communicated successfully in pairs or small groups, they will feel more confident about sharing with the class.

Let students control the all-class comprehension checks or discussions whenever possible. They can divide up the questions, assigning each one to a different student or pair of students working together. Use the board, and ask for a student volunteer to do the writing. For opinion questions, stress that there are no right or wrong answers. Encourage students to give their own ideas, and model acceptance of all opinions. For comprehension questions – as with vocabulary – give the answers yourself only as a last resort.

Give students plenty of time for discussion questions; circulate and encourage all students to voice their opinions. Whenever possible, pair and group students from different cultures. Move on to the next activity before discussion begins to die out or digress from the subject at hand.

Teacher's Role

As much as you can, try to take part as an equal in discussions and activities. Because so many of the tasks in this book are based on students' own knowledge and opinions, you should spend most of your time in the role of a participant or facilitator rather than authority figure. You will probably discover that the students are teaching you as much as you are teaching them.

Homework

Some of the activities in *Academic Listening Encounters* can be done at home. For example, students can read and then think or write about given discussion questions, and they can do the "Guessing Vocabulary from Context" task before the lecture. They can also do many of the After the Lecture tasks at home, using the notes they took while listening to the lecture. Interviews, research, and surveys are normally done outside of class time.

Encourage students to gain additional listening practice by listening at home to the chapter lectures that are on the audio CD in the back of the Student's Book. Depending on the level of the class, you may want students to listen either before or after you have played the lecture for them in class. If you think it will be helpful for students, you can also let them know that the listening script for the complete audio program is available at the *Academic Encounters* section of the Cambridge website, *www.cambridge.org/esl*.

Testing

The lecture in each chapter may be used as a listening and note-taking test. Quizzes on the content of the lectures are in the Lecture Quizzes section of this manual and may be photocopied for distribution to the students. Students may answer each quiz either on the quiz sheet or on their own paper. When taking the tests, students should refer only to the notes they took for the lecture tasks. Answers to the quizzes are in the last section of this manual, Lecture Quiz Answers.

Chapter-by-Chapter Teaching Suggestions and Answer Key

Belonging to a Group

Unit Title Page (Student's Book page 1)

Read the title of the unit aloud and elicit from students what it means to "belong to a group." Look at the photograph and discuss its relationship to the unit title.

Read the unit summary paragraph with students. Make sure students understand some of the key words that will be used in the unit: *behave, influence, peer pressure,* and *culture shock.* Chapter 1 deals with the ways the family group is changing over time and the implications of these changes, as well as some key ways in which it has remained essentially the same. Chapter 2 concerns other groups that we belong to, and it examines the role of peers. The second chapter also examines the meaning of culture and the phenomenon of culture shock. As this is the first unit in the book, review the structure of the chapters. Explain that in each chapter students will learn new information and practice their listening skills by listening to interviews and a lecture. Other tasks will help them refine their note-taking skills, and there are many opportunities to discuss the issues with their classmates. In Section 3, "In Your Own Voice," students will also have the opportunity to participate in an individual, group, or class project related to the topic of the chapter.

Chapter 1

Marriage, Family, and the Home

Look at the two photographs and discuss their relationship to the chapter title and the chapter description on the unit title page.

1 GETTING STARTED (Student's Book pages 2–3)

The introductory paragraph presents a comparison between the family group of today and the family group of the past. Read it with the students and make sure that they understand the word *contemporary*.

READING AND THINKING ABOUT THE TOPIC

This short passage introduces the concept of the *nuclear family* and goes on to list several key influences that are making it increasingly less common in the industrialized world. Terms that may need clarification include *nuclear family*, *far-reaching social changes*, *industrialization*, *cohabitation*, and *alternative family structures*.

Answers to step 2 (Student's Book page 3)

1 The "traditional nuclear family" refers to two married adults who live together and take care of their children.

2 The word *family* is hard to define today because of the far-reaching social changes of the past century.

3 Influences on the family structure include industrialization, more geographic mobility, and women's progress toward equal rights.

🎧 LISTENING FOR NUMERICAL INFORMATION

Give students adequate time to read the questions and answers in the table. If you wish, you can present the questions first, and allow students to guess the answers before they read the material. Because this information concerns the United States and thus may differ in regard to students' countries of origin, offer students the opportunity to share their different cultural perspectives about the content: divorce rates, single-parent families, family size, cohabitation, and living alone.

Answers to step 2 (Student's Book page 3)
1 False. About 50% of all U.S. marriages end in divorce.
2 True.
3 False. The average size of families in the United States is three people or fewer.
4 True.
5 False. About one in ten households consists of only one person.

2 AMERICAN VOICES: Robert and Carlos (Student's Book pages 4–8)

Make sure that students understand the terms *extended family* and *single-parent home*.

BEFORE THE INTERVIEWS
PERSONALIZING THE TOPIC

The three questions in step 1, which concern family composition, family characteristics, and family lessons, lead into the experiences of the interviewees. Take time to allow students to share the information about their own families with their partners in both steps 1 and 2. If you wish, you can even ask students to write a short paragraph on their family background and share it with other class members.

INTERVIEW WITH ROBERT: Growing up in an extended family

Look at the picture of Robert. Read the vocabulary items in the box aloud, allocating time for questions about meaning, use, and pronunciation of each one.

🎧 LISTENING FOR DETAILS

As in all exercises, have students go over the questions before they listen and give them the opportunity to query vocabulary they may not know, such as *attitude, protective, teens, block, basement,* and *rebel*.

Answers to step 2 (Student's Book page 6)
1 a
2 b
3 a
4 b
5 b
6 b
7 b
8 a
9 b

INTERVIEW WITH CARLOS: Growing up in a single-parent family

Look at the picture of Carlos on page 7 of the Student's Book. Read the vocabulary items in the box aloud, allocating time for questions about meaning, use, and pronunciation of each one.

🎧 PARAPHRASING WHAT YOU HAVE HEARD

Discuss the key academic skill of paraphrasing. You might need to spend time defining this skill, explaining its importance, and differentiating it from quoting, retelling, and summarizing. You may want to review the task commentary box explanations for retelling (Student's Book page 103) and summarizing (Student's Book page 46) before you discuss paraphrasing with the students.

Sample answers to step 2 (Student's Book page 7)

Carlos grew up in a *single-parent* household. His parents moved from Puerto Rico to the United States when he was *five/five years old*, but his mother left his father shortly afterwards. His mother was a garment worker, and garment work is *seasonal*. Sometimes she needed to work a lot and left the children alone. When Carlos was older, he used to *play* with *his sister/neighborhood friends* after school until his mother got home from work.

Carlos' mother taught him two important lessons about life: to take *care of himself* and to get an education. As a child, he learned to *cook, clean, iron* and run errands. He also studied *Spanish* at home with his mother.

Carlos thinks that it is important for children to have someone in the family who is a kind of *positive influence/anchor* in their lives. He thinks children are also influenced by people outside the family. For example, he met a lot of good *teachers* when he was growing up who taught him many positive lessons.

AFTER THE INTERVIEWS

THINKING CRITICALLY ABOUT THE TOPIC

1 | Explain that this task is an opportunity for students to think critically about some of the changes in the family structure that they have heard about. In this first step of the process they will compare their own experiences to those of Robert and to those of Carlos.

2,3 | Encourage students to articulate their views about the positive and negative consequences of the changes in the American family.

The chart can be used in various ways, depending on time constraints and the needs of the class. Some teachers might prefer to assign it for homework; others might wish to divide the class into groups and assign one or more of the changes in the American family per group for a more detailed and collaborative response.

IN YOUR OWN VOICE (Student's Book page 9)

GIVING ORAL PRESENTATIONS

The task in this section asks students to prepare a short oral presentation in front of the class. Some students may find this difficult: stronger students can be pushed to prepare a longer or more detailed response to one of the topics, or to hand in a written version of what they say.

Read through the commentary box guidelines with the students. Stress the point that speaking in front of a class is a common practice in most English-speaking countries, such as the United States, and that since they are speaking about their own families, they are truly experts on the subject and have valuable ideas to contribute.

4 ACADEMIC LISTENING AND NOTE TAKING: Family Lessons

(Student's Book pages 10–16)

This lecture concerns the best way to teach children appropriate behavior, and it is likely to fuel class discussion and provoke disagreement.

BEFORE THE LECTURE

PERSONALIZING THE TOPIC

Having pairs present their ideas aloud will promote listening and speaking practice.

NOTE TAKING: LISTENING FOR MAIN IDEAS AND SUPPORTING DETAILS

This basic note-taking skill is the first one introduced in the book. Read through the commentary box with the students. Explain that the more practice they get in listening to academic lectures, the more familiar they will become with the various phrases lecturers use to introduce supporting details.

The purpose of asking students to distinguish between ordinary, or personal, examples and academic references is so they understand that supporting details in an academic lecture are not necessarily restricted to research and statistics, although these are important. Understanding this point will help students to see the value of their own personal experiences and knowledge.

Answers to step 1 (Student's Book page 11)

	Example	Academic reference
1 Children learn good behavior through rewards.	☐	✔
2 Another way children learn to behave is through punishments.	✔	☐
3 Parents can teach children by modeling appropriate behavior.	✔	☐
4 "Don't do as I do. Do as I tell you," doesn't usually work.	☐	✔
5 Parents worry about negative lessons.	☐	✔

LECTURE, Part One: Rewards and Punishments

GUESSING VOCABULARY FROM CONTEXT

Read through the commentary box with students and explain how critical this skill is for their progress in English.

It is extremely important whenever students do this task that they take the time to do step 1 before proceeding to step 2. Explain to students that they may not be able to guess the meaning of every vocabulary item from the context, but if they continue to try, their ability will increase significantly.

Answers to step 2 (Student's Book page 12)

1 f
2 e
3 g
4 c
5 b
6 i
7 j
8 a
9 h
10 d

NOTE TAKING: ORGANIZING YOUR NOTES IN COLUMNS

Read through the task commentary box with the students, emphasizing the importance of organizing notes in a clear way that will allow them to retrieve the information later.

Advise students that they should read the instructions for all the steps in the task before beginning.

In step 2, it is important that students take notes on their own paper, though whether their notes for this step are in columns or organized in some other way doesn't matter. In this task and all subsequent note-taking tasks, be sure that students take complete notes on their own paper and then use those notes to do the task. It is essential that students practice taking their own notes, even though they may have difficulty at first. (Note that the quizzes in the back of this manual instruct students to use only the information from their own notes in their answers.)

Point out to students that their notes should always include the name of the lecture and the lecturer, as illustrated in the sample notes throughout the book. You might also want to suggest that they include the date of the lecture.

In step 4, it is important to remind students that their notes do not have to be identical to those of other students.

<table>
<tr><td colspan="2">Ms. Beth Handman: Family Lessons
Part One: Rewards and Punishments</td></tr>
<tr><td>Main Ideas</td><td>Details</td></tr>
</table>

Main Ideas	Details
1 Type of family (traditional or nontraditional) is not as important as love and support at home.	
2 Three ways children learn social behavior from their families: rewards, punishments, modeling	
3 Children learn good behavior through rewards.	• defined as pos. reinforcement for good behavior • eat vegetables – then ice cream • finish homework – then TV • children get gifts for good behavior
4 Another way children learn to behave is through punishments.	• second important way that children are socialized • Parents stop children from going out with friends if they do something wrong. • Parents don't let children watch TV if they get bad grades.
5 Rewards and punishments are controversial.	• Some rewards are not necessary: like bribes. (Take out garbage, get cookie) • Hitting on hand/spanking doesn't teach children anything. • If parents are violent, children may become violent.

LECTURE, Part Two: Modeling

GUESSING VOCABULARY FROM CONTEXT

Answers to step 2 (Student's Book page 14)

1 e
2 d
3 b
4 a
5 f
6 c

🎧 NOTE TAKING: ORGANIZING YOUR NOTES IN COLUMNS

Have the students read the instructions for all the steps before they begin. Be sure they take complete notes on their own paper in step 2.

Ms. Beth Handman: Family Lessons	
Part Two: Modeling	
Main Ideas	**Details**
6 Modeling means: <u>learning to behave by following an example.</u>	
7 <u>First role models are often parents.</u>	• Peter likes to study because his <u>mother studies with him.</u>
8 "Don't do as I do, <u>do as I tell you</u>" doesn't work.	• Studies: <u>If you smoke, probably ineffective to tell a child not to smoke.</u>
9 Modeling is the most important way children learn.	• Children have many models: <u>family members, friends, babysitters, professionals in childcare centers, each other, TV</u>
10 Parents worry about negative lessons.	• <u>from other children</u> • <u>from TV: 80% of programs contain violent behavior</u>
11 Most important thing: <u>grow up in environment with fair rules that are followed</u>	

AFTER THE LECTURE

THINKING CRITICALLY ABOUT THE TOPIC

Give students adequate time to discuss the questions. Prompt them to be sure to answer the last question: "Why?" If there is time, elicit a few answers to share with the class.

SHARING YOUR OPINION

Read through the commentary box with students. Point out that discussions usually involve sharing your opinion, even if that instruction is not specifically stated.

Childcare is one of the most complex issues facing families with young children and is likely to provoke different reactions. As more and more women enter the workforce, childcare decisions are becoming much more pressing. Give students the opportunity to share stories about childcare arrangements in their own extended families and communities. You may wish to supplement the discussion with newspaper articles or on-line research.

Chapter 1 Lecture Quiz

See the Lecture Quiz section at the back of this manual for a photocopiable quiz on the lecture for Chapter 1. Quiz answers can be found on pages 137–141.

The Power of the Group

Look at the photograph and discuss its relationship to the chapter title and the chapter description on the unit title page.

1 GETTING STARTED (Student's Book pages 17–18)

READING AND THINKING ABOUT THE TOPIC

As students read, remind them that in Chapter 1 they considered the family group as one of the most important influences in a person's development, and now they are expanding their discussion to other groups that a person may belong to. Make sure they understand the terms *peers*, *expectations*, and *interactions*.

Answers to step 2 (Student's Book page 18)
1 The six groups mentioned are families, friends, work associates, school associates, people of the same nationality, and members of the same religious group.
2 Belonging to a group might influence our opinions about the world, the way we interact with others, and the decisions that we make.

LISTENING FOR SPECIFIC INFORMATION

The situations pinpoint the sometimes conflicting influences of family and of friends. Allow students to respond fully and elicit their own similar experiences.

Answers to step 2 (Student's Book page 18)
1 Rebecca would go to the wedding because of family pressure. Jim would not go.
2 Both Jim and Rebecca would go to the movie with friends.
3 Rebecca would try on the shoes; Jim would not.
4 Jim would not go away with his parents. Rebecca would not go, either.

11

Discuss the meaning of *peer* and *peer pressure* with students.

BEFORE THE INTERVIEWS

SHARING YOUR OPINION

Encourage students to explain the reasons for their answers.

PERSONALIZING THE TOPIC

Students might wish to discuss the experiences of their younger siblings or cousins in addition to their own. Some students might be parents themselves. Elicit students' opinions about parental rules.

INTERVIEW WITH HENRY: *Living with teenagers*

Look at the picture of Henry on page 20 of the Student's Book. Read the vocabulary items in the box aloud, allocating time for questions about meaning, use, and pronunciation of each one.

⌒ LISTENING FOR MAIN IDEAS

Make sure students understand that in steps 1 and 2 they are being asked to think about what other people say. In steps 3 and 4 they have a chance to give their own opinions.

Answers to step 2 (Student's Book page 20)
Henry's main ideas are that parents should monitor their children's behavior, give them freedom to experiment but be firm that they can't do illegal or dangerous things, and listen to the way they as parents talk to their children.

Answer to step 4, item 1 (Student's Book page 21)
Henry's point of view is expressed by the second statement: "As you get older, your family becomes less important to you and your friends become more important."

INTERVIEW WITH VICTOR AND SAMIRA: *The influence of peers*

Look at the pictures of Victor and Samira on page 21 of the Student's Book. Read the vocabulary items in the box aloud, allocating time for questions about meaning, use, and pronunciation of each one.

⌒ LISTENING FOR SPECIFIC INFORMATION

Make sure students preview the questions before listening so that they can maximize their comprehension.

Answers to step 2 (Student's Book page 22)
1 Victor is eleven; he says he will be twelve next month.
2 Victor agrees that his friends sometimes influence him, although he hesitates before responding.

3 Victor wants to get a video game like his friend Marcos.

4 His mother thinks it is a waste of money.

5 Victor is going to ask his father to persuade his mother to let him get the video game.

6 Samira is in the tenth grade.

7 She says her friends really influence her a lot, although she says that it is important for people to think for themselves and not to conform all the time.

8 Samira says that her friends influence her more than her parents.

AFTER THE INTERVIEWS

PERSONALIZING THE TOPIC

If students feel comfortable discussing their own upbringings, allow them to share their feelings, list the lessons their parents taught them, and describe moments of conflict. Students can also write narrative essays about their experiences.

EXAMINING GRAPHIC MATERIAL

Read through the task commentary box with the students. Discussing numbers and percentages can be challenging. If students need help expressing or pronouncing the percentages, take time to help them.

3 IN YOUR OWN VOICE (Student's Book page 23)

CONDUCTING A SURVEY

Explain that conducting a survey outside of class will provide valuable speaking and listening practice in English. Likewise, conducting a survey in an EFL environment has several benefits – it will allow for collecting ideas and then summarizing them in English.

Make sure that students understand the meaning of the word *fad* and help them make the link between a fad and peer or group pressure. Give them time to practice asking their questions with other classmates before they approach a person outside of class. Make sure that they understand the need to take detailed notes, either during the interview or immediately after it. Have them present their findings in a short presentation (3–4 minutes) and discuss any interesting vocabulary that arises.

This activity can be done in several ways. Students can conduct their survey and present their findings to the class individually or in pairs. Alternatively, individuals or pairs can conduct the survey and present their findings to a small group. Then each group can collate the information and one individual or pair from each group can present it to the class.

4 ACADEMIC LISTENING AND NOTE TAKING: Culture Shock – Group Pressure in Action (Student's Book pages 24–30)

Make sure students understand the meaning of *social sciences* and *cross-cultural studies*. Explain that they will learn more about the term *culture* in the first subsection, "Before the Lecture."

BEFORE THE LECTURE

BUILDING BACKGROUND KNOWLEDGE ON THE TOPIC

Answer any vocabulary questions that arise as students read the passage. Discuss why the iceberg is a good illustration of our ideas about culture.

Students should be encouraged to explain and discuss their reasons for placing each aspect of culture either above or below the water level.

You might suggest to students that they expand their background knowledge by doing research about Edward Hall or the iceberg model. A great deal of material on this subject is available online.

Sample answers for step 2 (Student's Book page 24)

Above the water level:
- our ideas about what looks fashionable
- names of popular musicians
- the kind of food that is sold in supermarkets

Below the water level:
- ways of showing emotion
- the ways older and younger people should behave
- the amount of physical distance we leave between ourselves and others when we have a conversation
- our ideas about what looks beautiful
- how late we can arrive at an appointment without being rude

STUDYING A SYLLABUS

Point out the importance of looking carefully at a lecturer's or instructor's syllabus. Ask if any of the students has ever experienced culture shock, and let them compare their experiences.

◠ NOTE TAKING: LISTENING FOR ORGANIZATIONAL PHRASES

Dividing a lecture or essay into an introduction, body, and conclusion is second nature to many English speakers, but it is not necessarily what students from other cultural backgrounds are used to doing. Review the organizational phrases with students and explain that these phrases can also be used for their written assignments.

Answers to step 3 (Student's Book page 26)
1 d (The subject of today's lecture is . . .)
2 b (I'm going to focus on three main ideas in this lecture. . . .)
3 f (First of all, we will consider . . .)
4 c (Secondly, I will describe . . .)
5 g (Finally, I'll mention . . .)

6 h (First, then, . . .)
7 a (Now let's turn to . . .)
8 e (To conclude, let's look at . . .)

LECTURE, Part One: Reasons for Culture Shock

GUESSING VOCABULARY FROM CONTEXT

Answers to step 2 (Student's Book page 27)

1 d
2 c
3 g
4 e
5 h
6 a
7 b
8 f

🎧 NOTE TAKING: ORGANIZING YOUR NOTES IN OUTLINE FORM

Remind students that they will learn several ways to organize their notes in this book. In Chapter 1 they practiced organizing their notes in columns. Here they practice a different method – outline form. Read through the commentary box with students. As with organizational phrases, organizing notes in outline form may not be a practiced skill for all students, so you might want to illustrate the form on the board.

Make sure students understand that they should take complete notes on their own paper first. Then they should fill in the missing parts of the outline from their notes.

Sample answers for step 3 (Student's Book page 28)

Professor Iván Zatz
Culture Shock – Group Pressure in Action

I Definition of culture shock = <u>the experience many people have when they travel to another country</u>

II 3 Main ideas
    A <u>Reasons why people experience culture shock</u>
    B <u>Different stages of culture shock</u>
    C Applications of culture-shock research

III Reasons for culture shock
    A one set of rules growing up – not often articulated
    B other countries – <u>governed by other rules</u>
    C can't use your own <u>culture as a map</u>
        1 people act <u>irrationally</u>
        2 people feel <u>shocked and out of control</u>

LECTURE, Part Two: Stages of Culture Shock

GUESSING VOCABULARY FROM CONTEXT

Answers to step 2 (Student's Book page 29)
1 d
2 h
3 a
4 g
5 c
6 i
7 f
8 e
9 b

🎧 NOTE TAKING: COPYING A LECTURER'S DIAGRAMS AND CHARTS

Have students copy the diagram and think ahead about the kind of information it might contain. Make sure students take notes on the entire second part of the lecture and then use their notes to fill in the missing information in the diagram.

Answers to step 2 (Student's Book page 30)
Stage 1: Honeymoon
    Emotions: euphoria, excitement, enthusiasm
Stage 2: Letdown
    Emotions: loneliness, confusion
Stage 3: Resignation
    Emotion: adjustment

After students have practiced giving an oral summary (step 4), you might want to ask them how they could add this information to their outline. Elicit that Roman numeral "IV" would be "Stages of culture shock," that the three stages would be capital letters, and the emotions would be Arabic numerals. Show students that because for the third stage, "Resignation," there is only one emotion, they should avoid having a lone "1" by doing something such as adding a dash (i.e., "C. Resignation – adjustment"). You can also ask students for suggestions about how to put the last portion of the lecture that concerns practical applications of culture shock into outline form. Write one or two of their suggestions on the board and evaluate them, guiding students toward a workable outline.

AFTER THE LECTURE

SHARING YOUR OPINION

If applicable, students may want to distinguish between what is acceptable or not in their native communities and their present communities.
    Some classes might find it interesting to assemble small travel guides.

Chapter 2 Lecture Quiz

See the Lecture Quiz section at the back of this manual for a photocopiable quiz on the lecture for Chapter 2. Quiz answers can be found on pages 137–141.

Additional Ideas for Unit 1

Some key topics in this unit include the changing family structure, parent-child relationships, socialization, group pressure, peer pressure during adolescence, culture shock, and cultural differences.

1 With your students, watch a movie about families and/or group pressure. Some movies that deal with these themes are *Igby Goes Down, My Big Fat Greek Wedding,* and *Stand by Me.*

2 Invite another teacher to class to give his or her perspective on the issue of rewards and punishments. Alternatively, invite a person who has lived in another country for a long period to share their perspective on culture shock.

3 Have students find current newspaper or magazine articles about childcare and changing family structure, or immigration and cultural adjustment. Discuss the articles in class or ask students to present short summaries of the articles to each other.

4 Together with the class, read an essay or short story about family relationships, peer pressure, or cultural identity. Some possibilities are "Four Generations" by Joyce Maynard, "Interpreter of Maladies" by Jhumpa Lahiri, and "Mother Tongue" by Amy Tan. Discuss the works in class.

5 Have students share stories about their travel experiences, international friendships, and cross-cultural insights.

Gender Roles

Unit Title Page (Student's Book page 31)

Read the title of the unit aloud. Be prepared for students to question how the meaning of *gender* differs from the meaning of *sex*. You might tell them this question is answered in the first task in Chapter 3, "Reading and Thinking about the Topic." If it becomes necessary to discuss the words' differences further at this point, you can explain that *gender* refers to the classification of human beings according to whether they are male or female. Sometimes the words *gender* and *sex* are used interchangeably. *Gender* is more often used to talk about socially-conditioned, typical behavior of males and females; *sex* is more often used to talk about physical characteristics. *Gender* is used instead of *sex* in some contexts because of the latter's meaning of *sexual relations*.

Look at the photographs and discuss their relationship to the unit title. Read the unit summary paragraph with students. Make sure students understand these key words: *raised, benefits,* and *gender equality.* Chapter 3 discusses how boys and girls learn gender roles. Chapter 4 concerns other gender issues, particularly issues of equality in the workplace and at home. Students might be asked to express some initial reactions to these topics or to tell their classmates about any gender issues that particularly interest them.

Chapter 3

Growing Up Male or Female

Look at the photograph and discuss its relationship to the chapter title and the chapter description on the unit title page.

1 GETTING STARTED (Student's Book pages 32–34)

READING AND THINKING ABOUT THE TOPIC

The passage explains the difference between *sex* and *gender* and describes the concept of gender roles. Ideas and terms that need attention include *socially learned patterns of behavior, explore their individuality,* and *pressure to conform.* Students may have strong reactions to these concepts.

Answers to step 2 (Student's Book page 33)
1 We learn about masculinity and femininity through the process of socialization.
2 Both boys and girls have more freedom today to explore their individuality and less pressure to conform to traditional gender roles.

PERSONALIZING THE TOPIC

Be prepared for the fact that the definitions in this task will necessarily involve overlap. For example, the distinctions between *friendly, kind,* and *nice* are quite subtle and perhaps subject to interpretation. Let students discuss these distinctions, if they arise, and offer your views.

Answers to the first part of step 1 (Student's Book page 33)
Athletic: is good at sports
Brave: is not afraid of doing things
Competitive: wants to be the best at things
Cooperative: works well with other people
Friendly: gets along well with other people
Independent: can make decisions alone
Mischievous: behaves badly
Passive: prefers to be led by others
Strong-willed: does what he or she wants to do
Timid: is afraid to talk to others; is shy

Sample answers to step 2 (Student's Book page 33)
Adventurous: likes to do new things, to have adventures
Aggressive: behaves in a strong, angry way
Cowardly: is afraid of doing things
Gentle: behaves in a soft, kind way
Helpful: likes to help others
Kind: does things to show care for other people
Nice: friendly and pleasant
Responsible: takes charge of things; does what is required or necessary
Sweet: kind, gentle, and friendly
Thoughtful: thinks about other people and their needs

BUILDING BACKGROUND KNOWLEDGE ON THE TOPIC

1 | Introduce this task with a discussion of children's poems or stories that students remember from their own childhood.

After students have discussed the illustrations in groups, have them share their thoughts as a class. It is very important that students understand as much as possible from the illustrations because they may have trouble at first making sense of the words of the rhymes.

2 | After students listen to the recorded material and before they fill in the chart, discuss with them what they understood from their listening. You might want to write out the words of the nursery rhymes on the board and discuss any vocabulary students don't understand.

Sample answers to step 2 (Student's Book page 34)
1 "What Are Children Made Of?"
       Girls: nice, sweet, gentle
       Boys: adventurous
2 "Jack Be Nimble"
       Boys: athletic, adventurous
3 "Polly, Put the Kettle On"
       Girls: helpful, friendly, cooperative, thoughtful
4 "Little Miss Muffet"
       Girls: cowardly, timid
5 "Georgie Porgie"
       Girls: timid
       Boys: aggressive, mischievous

2 AMERICAN VOICES: Linda and Shingo (Student's Book pages 35–39)

Read through the introductory paragraph with students. Remind them that *raised* and *upbringing* are words they encountered in Chapter 1 in relation to Robert and Carlos and that these words have the same meaning in both contexts.

BEFORE THE INTERVIEWS

PERSONALIZING THE TOPIC

> If there is time, let students have the opportunity to explain their experiences and viewpoints in small groups or with the whole class. Some vocabulary items might need explanation, such as *chores, garbage, crayons, overalls,* and *jewelry.*

INTERVIEW WITH LINDA: Bringing up a son

Look at the picture of Linda on page 37 of the Student's Book. Read the vocabulary items in the box on page 36 aloud, allocating time for questions about meaning, use, and pronunciation of each one.

Ask students what might be difficult about bringing up a son in society today.

⌒ ANSWERING MULTIPLE-CHOICE QUESTIONS

> Review the directions with students and clarify that in this exercise they are being asked to mark the two correct answers and cross out the incorrect one. Discuss how students can focus their listening in order to do this. One way is to circle or put a check by the things they hear Linda say; then, the other answer must be wrong. The exercise can be done in the opposite way, too. Students can mark the answer they *do not* hear, thus indicating the other two are correct. You might pair students up before they listen and suggest that one partner listen for the correct answers and the other partner "listen" for the incorrect answer.
>
> Students should preview the questions carefully before listening to the interview.

> **Answers to step 2** (Student's Book page 37)
> **1** correct: a, c   incorrect: b
> **2** correct: a, b   incorrect: c
> **3** correct: a, b   incorrect: c
> **4** correct: b, c   incorrect: a
> **5** correct: b, c   incorrect: a
> **6** correct: a, c   incorrect: b
> **7** correct: b, c   incorrect: a

INTERVIEW WITH SHINGO: Growing up as a boy or girl

Look at the picture of Shingo on page 37 of the Student's Book. Read the vocabulary items in the box aloud, allocating time for questions about meaning, use, and pronunciation.

🎧 LISTENING FOR SPECIFIC INFORMATION

Preview the statements about the way parents can treat their sons and daughters. Discuss how differences or similarities in the way boys and girls are raised is affected by many factors, such as personal choice and societal expectations. Allow students to share any personal anecdotes.

Answers to step 2 (Student's Book page 38)

1 B
2 S
3 S
4 D
5 D
6 D
7 D
8 N

AFTER THE INTERVIEWS

DRAWING INFERENCES

Review the commentary box with students and explain the importance of understanding what is inferred as well as what is actually said. Try to elicit from students examples of instances where something is meant but not explicitly stated. You might ask students to think of examples in which what a teacher meant and what students understood were different.

Remind students that they should be prepared to support their opinions with evidence.

SHARING YOUR OPINION

Ask students to contribute their opinions, and to add other examples of their own.

3 IN YOUR OWN VOICE (Student's Book pages 40–41)

CONDUCTING AND PRESENTING YOUR OWN RESEARCH

Students are asked to replicate an experiment about gender expectations. If students feel uncomfortable doing this experiment, ask them to work with another student who does not. In each group, one student is the "actor" who models a kind of behavior that is more commonly associated with the other sex, and other students act as observers.

After students present their findings, ask them to reevaluate their ideas on gender roles and how those roles are interpreted in society. If you wish, ask them to write a short reaction to the experiment.

RESPONDING TO PRESENTATIONS

In this task, students are asked to respond to the content and organization of a presentation. In Chapter 4, they will have the opportunity to respond to the style of a presentation, that is, the way in which the presenter delivers his or her information. It is important to help students understand that practicing this task will help each of them and that being evaluated does not make the task a "test."

Read through the commentary box with students and then guide them through the task as necessary.

Be sure that students make their own charts for each presentation or you can make a chart on an 8 1/2 x 11 sheet of paper and provide copies for the students.

Allow sufficient time for the listeners to take notes and to write their questions and comments before they share their responses with the presenters.

4 ACADEMIC LISTENING AND NOTE TAKING: The Benefits of Single-Sex Education for Girls (Student's Book pages 42–48)

Many students may not agree with Dr. Frosch's position. Remind them that they will not and should not necessarily agree with everything they hear or read. They should, however, pay careful attention and understand the points of the argument being made. The better they understand the points supporting an argument with which they disagree, the better they will be able to prepare an opposing argument. After the lecture, in the task "Thinking Critically about the Topic" on page 48, students will have the opportunity to practice arguing for and against statements related to the topic.

BEFORE THE LECTURE

BUILDING BACKGROUND KNOWLEDGE ON THE TOPIC

Read the passage aloud with the students. You might want to ask students to practice paraphrasing by putting the ideas in the passage into their own words. Allow volunteers to give their paraphrases. Discuss whether each paraphrase is accurate or whether it could be improved upon.

Look at the illustration and discuss its relationship to the passage.

Answers to step 2 (Student's Book page 42)

1 *Coeducational* means that boys and girls are taught together in the same classroom.

2 According to the passage, boys get more attention than girls, are given more demanding academic challenges, and are subjected to higher expectations. Girls are encouraged to be quiet and well behaved.

3 Answers will vary.

⌕ NOTE TAKING: USING SYMBOLS AND ABBREVIATIONS

Read through the commentary box with students. Allow time for students to absorb the information in the box. Emphasize that because symbols and abbreviations are used to make note taking easier, students should feel free to devise their own.

You might want to elicit symbols and abbreviations that students already use.

Answers to step 1 (Student's Book page 44)

1 c
2 j
3 l
4 i
5 a
6 m
7 k
8 f
9 n
10 b
11 d
12 g
13 h
14 e

LECTURE, Part One: Disadvantages and Advantages of Single-Sex Education for Girls

GUESSING VOCABULARY FROM CONTEXT

Answers to step 2 (Student's Book page 45)

1 g
2 d
3 e
4 b
5 f
6 a
7 c

🎧 NOTE TAKING: USING SYMBOLS AND ABBREVIATIONS

Sample answers to step 3 (Student's Book page 45)

> Dr. Mary Frosch: The Benefits of Single-Sex Education for Girls
>
> Part One: Disadvantages and Advantages
> of Single-Sex Education for Girls
>
> <u>Cons</u>
> - old fashioned –
>   ed. opps. diff. for ♂ & ♀
> - ♂/♀ can't dev. ability to interact/be
>   comfortable/compete
> - no smooth transition into adult
>   ♂/♀ world
>
> <u>Pros</u> (Dr. F. pro s-s ed.)
> - values ♀'s unique quals.
> - helps ♀'s dev. self-conf.

LECTURE, Part Two: Two Main Benefits of All Girls' Schools

GUESSING VOCABULARY FROM CONTEXT

Answers to step 2 (Student's Book page 46)

1 f
2 a
3 g
4 c
5 b
6 e
7 d

NOTE TAKING: USING YOUR NOTES TO WRITE A SUMMARY

Read through the commentary box with students. Then be sure that students do each of the steps in the task, not just the final one (step 4) of completing the summary. Students should understand that this task stresses both the importance of being able to write a good summary and the importance of taking good notes to refer to when writing a summary.

Sample answers to step 4 (Student's Book page 47)

The Benefits of Single-Sex Education for Girls
Part Two: Two Main Benefits of All Girls' Schools
Dr. Mary Frosch

Single-sex education <u>values</u> girls' unique qualities and also helps girls develop <u>self-confidence</u>.

    The unique qualities of girls include their ability to concentrate on <u>abstract</u> thinking at an <u>earlier</u> age than boys and their ability to <u>work</u> for longer periods of time. They also enjoy working in groups and teams. Girls are not as competitive as boys, but they tend to be <u>kind and cooperative</u>.

    Boys can be noisy and girls often react by becoming timid and losing their <u>self-esteem</u>. When they learn without the <u>distraction</u> of boys, girls feel confident in themselves, they enjoy being <u>leaders</u>, they help each other, and they freely ask for <u>help</u> if they don't understand something. In single-sex schools, girls can develop deep confidence in themselves. This self-confidence prepares them to become adults.

THINKING CRITICALLY ABOUT THE TOPIC

The "hot seat" is a good activity for promoting fluency and critical thinking. One student at a time sits in the "hot seat" and defends a particular viewpoint. Other students try to argue against the viewpoint. The results can be interesting because students may have to argue a position they do not agree with and this can result in their changing their minds, or at least appreciating the counterargument.

Adequate preparation for this activity is very important. Allow time for students to develop as many arguments as possible to support or refute the statements in step 1. Then group students in threes or fours. If you choose, you can put quieter students together so that they are not afraid to speak up.

Chapter 3 Lecture Quiz

See the Lecture Quiz section at the back of this manual for a photocopiable quiz on the lecture for Chapter 3. Quiz answers can be found on pages 137–141.

Chapter 4

Gender Issues Today

Look at the two photographs and discuss their relationship to the chapter title and the description of the chapter on the unit title page.

1 GETTING STARTED (Student's Book pages 49–51)

READING AND THINKING ABOUT THE TOPIC

The issue of gender equality is prominent in sociology today, and most students will be able to find some aspect of the topic to relate to. The passage discusses the progress that has been made and the problems still to be dealt with. Key terms include *feminist movement, household chores, equal rights,* and *serious issue.*

Answers to step 2 (Student's Book page 50)

1 Women made progress toward gaining equal opportunities in education. More women also entered the workforce. Girls were allowed to choose careers they wanted, not just those traditionally identified with their gender. Husbands began to share household chores and childcare with their wives.

2 Boys, as well as girls, were encouraged to choose careers they wanted, even if they were untraditional. Husbands began to share household chores and childcare with their wives.

3 Sociologists believe that progress has been made, but the problem of gender inequality is still a serious issue.

EXAMINING GRAPHIC MATERIAL

Look at the chart showing gains women made in various professions from 1975 to 2000 with students. Make sure that students understand the profession titles. They also need to review vocabulary for describing charts and graphs.

Answers to step 2 (Student's Book page 51)

1 Of the professions noted in this chart, women made the most gains in becoming economists. They also made some gains in becoming dentists, mail carriers, and physicians, and they made gains in the legal field.

2 Answers may vary. (It is interesting that women still hold the great majority of positions as childcare workers, nurses, and elementary school teachers. Note, too, that the number of women in computer programming has remained about the same.)

⌒ LISTENING FOR SPECIFIC INFORMATION

Answers to step 3 (Student's Book page 51)

Situation 1: If the employee is a man, people think he will work harder. If the employee is a woman, people think she will have a baby and leave her job.

Situation 2: If the employee is a man, people think: "He loves his family." If the employee is a woman, people think that she is more interested in her husband and children than she is in her career.

Situation 3: If the employee is a man, people think he is discussing something important. If the employee is a woman, people think she is just chatting.

Situation 4: If the employee is a man, people think the trip will be good for his career. If the employee is a woman, people wonder what her husband will think.

2 AMERICAN VOICES: Belinda and Farnsworth

(Student's Book pages 52–57)

Read through the introductory paragraph with students. Be sure that students understand the term *social worker*: someone who provides social services, such as economic and psychological aid, to those members of society requiring such aid – usually people with relatively low incomes.

BEFORE THE INTERVIEWS

BUILDING BACKGROUND INFORMATION ON THE TOPIC

1 | Read through the instructions, which explain *metaphor*, with students. Then read through the list of metaphors and their definitions below the illustration. Allow time for students to examine the illustration and see which of the listed metaphors it illustrates.

2 | **Answers to step 2** (Student's Book page 53)

1 e
2 d
3 f
4 b
5 a
6 c

3 | After students have completed step 3, you might want to expand on the concept of metaphor by eliciting from them other metaphors that they know, not necessarily about the workplace.

INTERVIEW WITH BELINDA: Gender discrimination in the workplace

Look at the picture of Belinda on page 54 of the Student's Book. Read the vocabulary items in the box on page 53 aloud, allocating time for questions about meaning, use, and pronunciation of each one.

🎧 ANSWERING MULTIPLE-CHOICE QUESTIONS

Make sure students understand that in this task they need only choose the one correct answer.

Answers to step 2 (Student's Book page 54)

1 c
2 b
3 c
4 b

INTERVIEW WITH FARNSWORTH: Gender inequality at home and in the workplace

Look at the picture of Farnsworth on page 55 of the Student's Book. Read the vocabulary items in the box on pages 54–55 aloud, allocating time for questions about meaning, use, and pronunciation of each one.

🎧 ANSWERING TRUE/FALSE QUESTIONS

Read through the commentary box with students. Make sure they understand the explanation of why true/false questions can sometimes be tricky.

Answers to step 2 (Student's Book page 55)

1 F
2 F
3 T
4 F
5 F
6 T
7 T

AFTER THE INTERVIEWS

THINKING CRITICALLY ABOUT THE TOPIC

Give students time to come up with feasible solutions to the four problems involving work and childcare. When pairs of students have a good solution, have them present it to the class. Compare the different solutions that are proposed and, as a class, examine the pros and cons of each of them.

EXAMINING GRAPHIC MATERIAL

Help students to describe the information they see in the graph, using the sentence structures in the box in step 2. Provide additional vocabulary support, if needed. Prompt a full answer to the inferential question about why women earn less than men.

3 IN YOUR OWN VOICE (Student's Book pages 58–59)

CONDUCTING AN INTERVIEW

This section asks students to interview people outside of class about problems faced by fathers who want to take a more active role in childcare. First, students are asked to do some library or on-line research on the topic so that they have a sense of the problem that they will be examining.

Guide the students as they do their initial research. Allow class time to review interesting material they locate. Help students narrow down their interview questions and find a good interview topic that interests them and that they know something about.

Make sure that students interview at least three people outside of class. If you wish, you can ask students to do a writing assignment on the topic.

GIVING FEEDBACK ON A PRESENTER'S STYLE

In Chapter 3 students practiced responding to the content of presentations. In this task, students practice giving feedback on the presenter's style. Notice, however, that the "preparation and organization" section of the model chart provides opportunity for response to the content of the presentation, although in a slightly different way than that in Chapter 3.

Read through the commentary box with the students. Be sure they understand that the purpose of this task is to help each student understand what he or she is doing well and to help him or her with suggestions for anything that needs improvement. As students practice evaluating each other, they will become more aware of the elements of style that they need to focus on when they present information. Stress the fact that constructive, fair, and respectful criticism can help the presenter make improvements and enrich the class discussion.

Review the questions found in the chart with students. As in Chapter 3, students can make their own charts or you can make one on an 8 1/2 x 11 sheet of paper and provide copies for the students.

Be sure that students have enough time to fill out their charts before sharing their feedback with the presenters.

4 ACADEMIC LISTENING AND NOTE TAKING: Gender and Language (Student's Book pages 60–64)

You may need to explain that *linguistics* is the study of human speech.

BEFORE THE LECTURE

BUILDING BACKGROUND KNOWLEDGE ON THE TOPIC

1 | Read the passage about gender-specific and gender-neutral language with the students, and discuss any problems they may have with the concepts. The passage is deliberately provocative when it refers to doctors, shoppers, and secretaries as "he."

Many students are concerned about correct use of pronouns and may have questions about accuracy. Be prepared for students to question you about your own use of pronouns and gender-neutral language.

2 | **Answers to step 2** (Student's Book page 60)

1 A "gender-specific" term is a term like *chairman,* which implies that this position is usually or always held by a man.

2 A "gender-neutral" term is a term like *chair,* which can be used to avoid indicating the sex of the individual in the position.

3 It is difficult to be gender-neutral when using pronouns because there is no gender-neutral singular pronoun in English.

4 The pronouns indicate that the doctor, the secretary, and the shopper are all male.

Encourage students to think of examples for items 1 and 2 other than those terms found in the reading passage.

🎧 NOTE TAKING: USING TELEGRAPHIC LANGUAGE

Read through the commentary box with students. Discuss how telegraphic language is often used in newspaper headlines to communicate the main idea quickly. If possible, bring in some sample headlines to show students.

Answers to step 2 (Student's Book page 61)

3	a
4	b
1	c
2	d

Sample answers to step 3 (Student's Book page 61)

a Topic: sexism in lang. & how to avoid it

b Many gen-spec. words: e.g., mailman, policeman

c "Mankind" = only men. "Human beings/people" = men & women

d Words affect thought. Ex: kids hear "chair<u>man</u>" & so think all must be <u>men</u>.

LECTURE, Part One: Gender-Specific and Gender-Neutral Language

GUESSING VOCABULARY FROM CONTEXT

Answers to step 1 (Student's Book pages 61–62)

1 a
2 c
3 c
4 b

🎧 NOTE TAKING: USING TELEGRAPHIC LANGUAGE

Sample answers to step 3 (Student's Book page 63)

Prof. Wendy Gavis: Gender and Language
Pt 1: Gender-Specific and Gender-Neutral Language

I   Main idea: Sexism in lang. & how to avoid it

II   Gen-spec lang.
    A   Def: Terms that refer to men
    B   Ex:
       1   mail   *man*
       2   police   "
       3   chair   "

III   Gen-neutral lang. shows
    A   World as is – ♀ can have same jobs as ♂ (Ex: mail carrier & police officer & chair)
    B   Equality (Ex: "human beings/people" not "mankind.")

IV   Grammar = problem
    A   Choices
       1   Everyone pick up *his* pen.
       2   "   "   "   her pen.
       3   "   "   "   their pen.
    B   Gavis uses their – not gram., but solves prob.
    C   Many univ. profs / writers / prob do same.

LECTURE, Part Two: Questions and Answers

GUESSING VOCABULARY FROM CONTEXT

Answers to step 2 (Student's Book page 63)

1 e
2 a
3 g
4 f
5 c
6 b
7 h
8 d

NOTE TAKING: USING TELEGRAPHIC LANGUAGE

2 You may want to have students take turns putting examples of their notes taken in telegraphic language on the board until you have a complete set of notes for Part Two of the lecture on the board in telegraphic language.

To emphasize that there is no standard way to write telegraphic language, you could elicit some variations and also write those on the board.

3 **Sample answers to step 3** (Student's Book page 64)

1 Gavis says that the language question is very important and is treated as a serious issue by international organizations. The issue concerns not just the words but the ideas behind them. For example, children's literature often shows boys having fun while girls stay in the background. Gavis believes that this kind of thinking has a bad effect on women.

2 Gavis says that the way we speak does have an influence on the way we think. According to Gavis, if a child grows up hearing the word *chairman* over and over again, that child will grow up thinking that only men can hold positions of authority.

3 Gavis says that the issue is receiving more and more attention worldwide. She notes that each language has its own gender issues.

AFTER THE LECTURE

APPLYING WHAT YOU HAVE LEARNED

1 Read through the commentary box with students. Emphasize that what they learn in the classroom is meant to be applied in all aspects of life, not only in answers to test questions.

Elicit responses about the meaning of the cartoon and why it is humorous.

2 **Sample answers to step 2** (Student's Book page 64)

> According to an article I just read, the quality of a university does not just depend on the teachers, but on the students. The teachers have to make sure their lessons are challenging and stimulating. But the students are also responsible for doing their homework, bringing their ideas to the classroom discussions, and contributing their opinions on the topic. They must make sure that they are not being passive, but are making full use of the opportunities that are being offered to them at the university. For example, the students should be ready to join clubs and participate with their classmates on special projects. They can also learn a lot by having [omit the article a] jobs that will bring them into contact with all the members of the university. These activities also contribute to a successful college experience.

Chapter 4 Lecture Quiz

See the Lecture Quiz section at the back of this manual for a photocopiable quiz on the lecture for Chapter 4. Quiz answers can be found on pages 137–141.

Additional Ideas for Unit 2

Some key topics in this unit include changing gender roles, the nature/nurture debate, parental expectations, single-sex/coeducation, gender discrimination at home and at work, and sexism in language.

1 With your students, watch a movie about gender roles or gender discrimination and discuss it in class. Some movies that deal with these themes are *Baby Boom, Billy Elliot,* and *Bend It Like Beckham.*

2 Have students conduct informal out-of-class interviews about changing gender roles. They should report back to the class with stories that they are told. Alternatively, visit a coeducational school or single-sex school and interview teachers about the learning styles of boys and girls.

3 With the class, read an essay or short story about gender roles. Some possibilities are: "Cinematypes" by Susan Allen Toth, "How to Get Out of a Locked Trunk" by Philip Weiss, and "No Name Woman" by Maxine Hong Kingston.

4 Have students share stories about the way they and their siblings were raised or share fairy tales and nursery rhymes from different countries.

5 Do on-line research about gender issues and workplace inequality and share the results of the research with the class.

Media and Society

Unit Title Page (Student's Book page 65)

Read the title of the unit aloud and elicit from students what they think the term *media* means. Then read through the paragraph with students. You can point out that *media* refers to channels of communication and the term *mass media* refers to channels of communication that reach a large public audience (the *mass* of the population). Note that *media* is the plural of *medium* and that it is used interchangeably with *channel* when we refer to a *medium* (or *channel*) *of communication*. Although grammatically the word *media* is a plural form, it is often used as a singular word (followed by a singular verb form), meaning all parts of the media industry taken as a whole.

Look at the collage of photographs and discuss its relationship to the unit title. Read the unit summary paragraph with students. Make sure students understand some of the key words and phrases that will be used in the unit: *news coverage, strengths and weaknesses,* and *insight.* Chapter 5 examines the volume and quality of news we get from various sources. Chapter 6 concerns the influence of newer forms of media; it discusses their benefits, as well as their possibly dangerous effects on society.

Chapter 5

Mass Media Today

Look at the photograph and discuss its relationship to the chapter title and the chapter description on the unit title page.

1 GETTING STARTED (Student's Book pages 66–67)

READING AND THINKING ABOUT THE TOPIC

The introductory passage discusses the rise in importance of the mass media. It also presents questions about its value. It is important for students to understand the following words and phrases: *shortened, far away, awareness, growth, raises questions, inaccurate,* and *one-sided.*

Answers to step 2 (Student's Book page 67)
1 The modern world is connected by rapid transportation, electronic communication, and the mass media.
2 The mass media allows information to be communicated quickly throughout the world.
3 Some people think that the information provided by the mass media might be inaccurate, one-sided, or incomplete.

🎧 LISTENING FOR SPECIFIC INFORMATION

Read the newspaper headlines with the students. Make sure they understand the terms *immigrants, cloning, mammals,* and *tornado.*

Answers to step 1 (Student's Book page 67)

7	**a**
1	**b**
6	**c**
2	**d**
8	**e**
3	**f**
4	**g**
5	**h**

2 AMERICAN VOICES: Carol, Shari, and Frank

(Student's Book pages 68–72)

Read the introductory paragraph with students. Elicit or explain what is meant by the term *mixed feelings*.

BEFORE THE INTERVIEWS

SHARING YOUR OPINION

Have students respond to the questions about the news independently before sharing their opinions with partners.

INTERVIEW WITH CAROL: Problems with TV news

Look at the picture of Carol on page 69 of the Student's Book. Read the vocabulary items in the box on pages 68 and 69 aloud, allocating time for questions about meaning, use, and pronunciation of each one.

⌒ ANSWERING MULTIPLE-CHOICE QUESTIONS

Answers to step 2 (Student's Book page 70)

1 c
2 b
3 a
4 b
5 b
6 c
7 b
8 b

INTERVIEW WITH SHARI AND FRANK: Reading the newspapers

Look at the pictures of Shari and Frank on page 71 of the Student's Book. Read the vocabulary items in the box on page 70 aloud, allocating time for questions about meaning, use, and pronunciation of each one.

1 | After students make their predictions, have a few volunteers explain the reasons for their predictions.

2 | **Answers to step 2** (Student's Book page 71)

    1 S
    2 F
    3 F
    4 S
    5 S
    6 F
    7 F
    8 S
    9 F
    10 S

AFTER THE INTERVIEWS

PARAPHRASING WHAT YOU HAVE HEARD

Before students begin this task, review the difference between a paraphrase and a summary by asking for a volunteer to explain it.

Sample answers (Student's Book page 71)

> Carol has very strong opinions about the news we get on TV. She thinks that it is more like entertainment than news. For example, serious stories about political problems and shallow stories, like plastic surgery, are presented in the same style. She believes that this is because we are used to instant gratification – something that doesn't require you to think. Newspapers and the Internet give better coverage, but it takes more time to find good articles, so Carol watches the news on TV.
>
> Shari gets her news from the Internet and newspapers. She thinks that the news is very negative. For example, there are stories about bombings and accidents. She also says that news in the United States is not as international as it is in Korea. Her favorite sections are arts and culture and she likes to read about people.
>
> Frank likes the newspaper. His favorite parts are sports and crosswords. He thinks you have to have your own opinions about the news, because it is usually biased.

SHARING YOUR OPINION

1 | Encourage students to take the time to give full answers to the questions.

2 | After students have been working in their groups for a while, elicit some sample responses.

3 IN YOUR OWN VOICE (Student's Book pages 73–74)

GIVING GROUP PRESENTATIONS

The purpose of this activity is to allow students to work together in a group and make a presentation in front of the class. Make sure that students understand the need to work collaboratively on the project and to distribute the work fairly among the group members. Give them adequate preparation time so that they can do on-line research, visit the library, and prepare any visual aids that they think will help their presentations.

If you wish, you can have class members evaluate the presentations using the techniques presented in "Responding to Presentations" (Chapter 3) and "Giving Feedback on a Presenter's Style" (Chapter 4).

4 ACADEMIC LISTENING AND NOTE TAKING: From Event to Story – Making It to the News (Student's Book pages 75–80)

Ask students what they know about newspapers and journalism. Perhaps some of them have written for school papers or have had written work published in some other way. Some students might even have parents, relatives, or friends who are journalists or professional writers. Allow them to share their knowledge and experience.

BEFORE THE LECTURE

PERSONALIZING THE TOPIC

Questions 1–3 do not have correct or incorrect answers; rather, they elicit students' opinions about the role of a newspaper as well as the responsibilities of journalists and the difficulties that they face. Allow time for students to give extensive answers to these questions. They might need time to think about how they want to respond.

After the students have had time to discuss the questions with their partners, you might want to elicit a few responses to share with the class.

THINKING CRITICALLY ABOUT THE TOPIC

1 | This activity asks students to compare coverage of an event in different newspapers. Students might need time to locate these articles, but they should be able to find them quickly if they have access to on-line resources.

2 | Make sure students understand the instructions and the questions for this step. Point out that they may not be able to answer these questions, at least not fully. The questions raise the difficult issues that all readers face as to the credibility of what they read.

🎧 NOTE TAKING: LISTENING FOR SIGNAL WORDS

Review the concept of signal words and explain that speakers often use them for a variety of reasons. Read through the commentary box with the students, making sure that they understand the meaning of the signal words and can pronounce them.

Answers to step 1 (Student's Book page 76)

1 c
2 e
3 f
4 a
5 b
6 d

Answers to step 2 (Student's Book page 76)

1 Nowadays
2 In fact
3 First of all
4 Sometimes
5 Usually
6 However

LECTURE, Part One: The Work of a Journalist

GUESSING VOCABULARY FROM CONTEXT

Answers to step 2 (Student's Book page 77)

1 c
2 b
3 d
4 i
5 e
6 g
7 f
8 h
9 a

⌒ NOTE TAKING: CHOOSING A FORMAT FOR ORGANIZING YOUR NOTES

It is important for students to realize that not everyone takes notes in the same way, at the same speed, and with the same ease. Some students will be able to take notes in a fairly well-organized format as they listen to a lecture. Others will take sloppy notes that have to be clearly organized afterwards. It is critical that students who cannot take well-organized notes as they listen get into the habit of organizing their notes as soon after the lecture as possible. Even those students who take fairly clear notes as they listen will undoubtedly be able to improve on their organization afterwards.

It is also important for students to experiment with the different note-taking formats presented in the Student's Book to see which one works best for them. You may, therefore, want to have students complete their notes in *both* formats: column and outline.

Sample answers to step 3: column format (continuation of notes on Student's Book page 78, Example 2a)

Planned events – can be anticipated	politician opening new store

Unplanned events
  – Ex: knife fight
    Rep's job =
	fire, crime
	
	go to scene
	get facts (what, when, where, who)
	interview witnesses (name, job, age)
	talk to ed.
	check facts

Sample answers to step 3: outline format (continuation of notes on Student's Book page 79, Example 2b)

III Planned events can be anticipated
     Ex: politician opening new store

IV Unplanned events
     Ex: fire, crime

V   Ex of reporter's job in unplanned event: knife fight
     A Go to scene
     B Get facts
         1 what
         2 when
         3 where
         4 who
     C Interview witnesses
         1 name
         2 job
         3 age
     D Talk to ed.
     E Check facts

LECTURE, Part Two: Getting a Story into Print

GUESSING VOCABULARY FROM CONTEXT

Answers to step 2 (Student's Book page 79)

1 c
2 a
3 e
4 d
5 f
6 b

After students have compared their notes with a partner, ask for a few volunteers to share their completed column-format notes and outline-format notes with the class. Choose at least two of each format. You can either photocopy the notes for each student (or pair of students) or put them on an overhead projector. Discuss the good things about each set of notes and talk about any places where they could be improved. (Refer to the Listening Script on page 101 of this manual for the content of Part Two of the lecture.)

AFTER THE LECTURE

APPLYING WHAT YOU HAVE LEARNED

Make sure that students understand on which day this task will be done and which newspaper they must bring to class. If necessary, explain the difference between early and late editions and tell them which one to get. You might consider having them get a newspaper from the previous day and reading it for homework.

You may prefer to have each group analyze one of the newspaper sections listed in the chart rather than all of them.

Chapter 5 Lecture Quiz

See the Lecture Quiz section at the back of this manual for a photocopiable quiz on the lecture for Chapter 5. Quiz answers can be found on pages 137–141.

The Influence of the Media

Look at the photograph and discuss its relationship to the chapter title and the chapter description on the unit title page.

1 GETTING STARTED (Student's Book pages 81–83)

Read the introductory paragraph with the students and allow them to express their opinions about the positive and negative effects of the media.

READING AND THINKING ABOUT THE TOPIC

Read the passage with students. Make sure they understand the words *expose* and *materialistic*.

Answers to step 2 (Student's Book page 82)
1 No, there is no agreement about exactly what the effects are.
2 Positive effects of TV are that it can entertain us, allow us to be better informed, and give us an increased understanding of the world. However, TV also exposes us to negative images and some critics argue that it can make us passive, violent, and materialistic.

PERSONALIZING THE TOPIC

Allow time for students to fill in the chart and share their responses. Encourage them to share their opinions about the various forms of entertainment.

43

⌒ RECORDING NUMERICAL INFORMATION

Read through the commentary box with students. Elicit from them what types of numerical information it is sometimes necessary to record in listening situations, such as telephone numbers, addresses, prices, and statistics in lectures.

Answers to step 2 (Student's Book page 83)
Area 1 (the United States, Canada, Europe, Australia, and Japan): 40 or more TVs per 100 people

Area 2 (Brazil, Russia, South Korea, and the People's Republic of China): Between 20 and 40 TVs per 100 people

Area 3 (Mexico, Central America, part of South America, part of Africa, and most of the Middle East): Between 8 and 20 TVs per 100 people

Area 4 (most of Africa and all of India): Fewer than 8 TVs per 100 people

2 AMERICAN VOICES: Eddie, Leslie, Ralph, Vanessa, Felix, and Richard (Student's Book pages 84–88)

This section presents the students with six mini-interviews on different aspects of the media.

BEFORE THE INTERVIEWS

PERSONALIZING THE TOPIC

As in all introductory activities, make sure that enough time is allocated for students to develop a personal viewpoint and articulate it to their partners before they listen to the interviews.

INTERVIEW WITH EDDIE, LESLIE, AND RALPH: Opinions about media

Look at the pictures of Eddie, Leslie, and Ralph on page 85 of the Student's Book. Read the vocabulary items in the box on pages 84 and 85 aloud, allocating time for questions about meaning, use, and pronunciation of each one.

⌒ LISTENING FOR SPECIFIC INFORMATION

Answers to step 1 (Student's Book page 85)
Eddie: video games
Leslie: cell phones
Ralph: (action) movies

Sample answers to step 2 (Student's Book pages 85–86)

Person	Positive effects	Negative effects
Eddie (video games)	Can be entertaining.	Some are violent. Have a wasteful effect, and stop kids from doing other activities, like reading. Can cause addiction. Could be dangerous for little kids. Make kids antisocial.
Leslie (cell phones)	Enable you to get in touch with people easily.	Are trendy and expensive. Are dangerous if used while driving.
Ralph (action movies)	Are interesting to watch. Movies where the hero catches the bad buy give a positive message.	Are violent and contain a lot of sex. Young kids think imaginary things that they see are real.

INTERVIEW WITH VANESSA, FELIX, AND RICHARD: Opinions about media

Look at the pictures of Vanessa, Felix, and Richard on page 87 of the Student's Book. Read the vocabulary items in the box on page 86 aloud, allocating time for questions about meaning, use, and pronunciation of each one.

🎧 LISTENING FOR SPECIFIC INFORMATION

Answers to step 1 (Student's Book page 87)

Vanessa: TV
Felix: TV
Richard: jet plane

Sample answers to step 2 (Student's Book page 87)

Person	Positive effects	Negative effects
Vanessa (TV)	X	TV news = infotainment, not real news. Treats war like video games.
Felix (TV)	Is very entertaining. Some programs (e.g., sports) give a positive message. Others are educational.	X (But parents have to monitor what children watch.)
Richard (jet plane)	FM radio is good for weather and music. Jet plane has improved international communication; allows travel and meeting people.	TV takes too much time. Modern technology destroys beauty and meaning in life. We become part of a machine.

AFTER THE INTERVIEWS

DRAWING INFERENCES

Read through the commentary box with the students.

The answers may vary. Encourage students to discuss their opinions openly – it does not matter if they disagree about the answers. (Refer to the Listening Script on pages 102–105 of this manual for the content of the interviews.)

THINKING CRITICALLY ABOUT THE TOPIC

Some classes may wish to organize a class debate around these statements. There is no correct answer to any of them, and students may openly disagree. Encourage them to express their views and to give support for their opinions.

3 IN YOUR OWN VOICE (Student's Book pages 89–90)

CONDUCTING AND PRESENTING YOUR OWN RESEARCH

The project that students are being asked to do here is a replica of an experiment originally designed by the sociologist Bernard McGrane. His work can be found on many Internet sites, and students might be interested in looking up some of the work he has published.

Students should follow the instructions closely and take careful notes on what they do and how they feel. The value of this exercise is in the self-analysis that accompanies the project.

4 ACADEMIC LISTENING AND NOTE TAKING: Dangers of the Mass Media (Student's Book pages 91–96)

BEFORE THE LECTURE

PERSONALIZING THE TOPIC

1 | Read through the passage with students and give them time to react to the information that is presented. Some of them may be amazed at the number of hours most TV sets are on.

2, 3 | Ask students to give honest responses to their use of the different media listed and to the purposes for which they use it. If time permits, you may want to open this discussion up to the class.

⌒ NOTE TAKING: ORGANIZING YOUR NOTES AS A MAP

Answers to step 2 (Student's Book page 92)

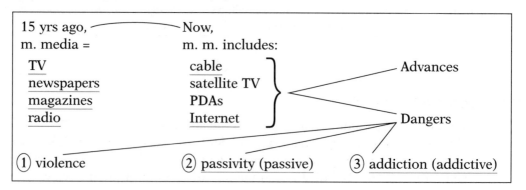

LECTURE, Part One: Issues of Violence, Passivity, and Addiction

GUESSING VOCABULARY FROM CONTEXT

Answers to step 2 (Student's Book page 93)

1 c
2 d
3 b
4 e
5 g
6 a
7 f

NOTE TAKING: ORGANIZING YOUR NOTES AS A MAP

Answers to step 1 and sample answers to step 2 (Student's Book pages 93–94)

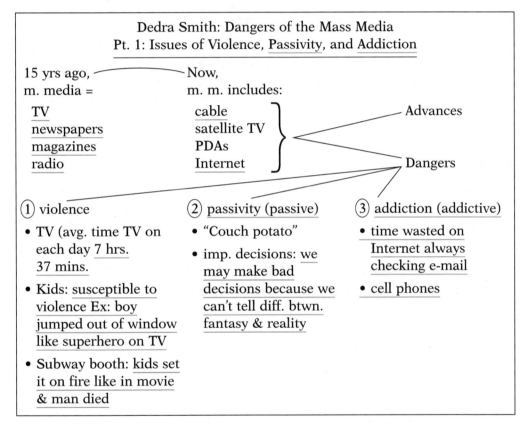

Dedra Smith: Dangers of the Mass Media
Pt. 1: Issues of Violence, Passivity, and Addiction

15 yrs ago,
m. media =

TV
newspapers
magazines
radio

Now,
m. m. includes:

cable
satellite TV
PDAs
Internet

Advances

Dangers

(1) violence

- TV (avg. time TV on each day 7 hrs. 37 mins.
- Kids: susceptible to violence Ex: boy jumped out of window like superhero on TV
- Subway booth: kids set it on fire like in movie & man died

(2) passivity (passive)

- "Couch potato"
- imp. decisions: we may make bad decisions because we can't tell diff. btwn. fantasy & reality

(3) addiction (addictive)

- time wasted on Internet always checking e-mail
- cell phones

LECTURE, Part Two: Issues of Advertising and Invasion of Privacy

GUESSING VOCABULARY FROM CONTEXT

Answers to step 2 (Student's Book page 94)

1 a
2 h
3 e
4 d
5 b
6 g
7 i
8 c
9 f

⌒ NOTE TAKING: ORGANIZING YOUR NOTES AS A MAP

Mapping is a particularly subjective approach to note taking. Therefore, it is important for students to understand that they have a choice – they can add to the map on page 93 of the Student's Book *or* they can make up a map with a different shape and put all the information from Parts One and Two of the lecture into it.

AFTER THE LECTURE

APPLYING WHAT YOU HAVE LEARNED

1 Read through the instructions with students. Discuss how hard it seems to believe initially that we are exposed to so many advertising messages. However, once students start to analyze their day, it should become evident that advertising is all around.

Sample answers to first part of step 1 (Student's Book pages 95–96)

Day in the life of a student	Marketing messages
6:30 Asleep	
7:00 Clock radio goes off; student stays in bed	Student hears several commercials
7:30 Gets up and showers	All toiletry products (shampoo, soap, etc.) have product name and sometimes advertise related products
7:50 Gets dressed	Clothes and shoes often have company logo
8:00 Eats breakfast	Breakfast cereals have product name and advertising messages; if radio is still on or if student turns on TV, he or she will hear more commercials
Etc.	

Chapter 6 Lecture Quiz

See the Lecture Quiz section at the back of this manual for a photocopiable quiz on the lecture for Chapter 6. Quiz answers can be found on pages 137–141.

Additional Ideas for Unit 3

Some key topics in this unit include different kinds of media and their importance in our lives, benefits and drawbacks of media, events of the last century, the role of journalism, and advertising.

1 With your class, watch a movie about the media, its advantages, and its dangers. Some movies that deal with these themes are *Ed TV*, *The Truman Show*, and *Bicentennial Man*.

2 Invite guests to talk to the class about their use of the media. Prepare for the visit by reviewing the unit and thinking of concerns and observations you can share with the visitor.

3 Read an essay or short story about the media and discuss it with the class. Some possibilities are "Remote Control: How to Raise a Media Skeptic" by Susan Douglas, "TV Isn't Violent Enough" by Mike Oppenheim, or "How to Write a Letter" by Garrison Keillor.

4 Have students share stories about the events that have shaped their countries or communities.

5 Do on-line research about media issues. Share the results of the research with the class.

Unit 4

Breaking the Rules

Unit Title Page (Student's Book page 97)

Read the title of the unit and discuss with students the meaning of "breaking the rules." Look at the photograph and discuss its relationship to the unit title. Read the unit summary paragraph with students. Make sure students understand some of the key terms that will be used in the unit: *concerned about, solving crime, prevent,* and *death penalty.* Chapter 7 looks at different types of crime, the people who commit crime, and those who are affected by crime. Chapter 8 examines ways that we can deal with crime in society, including different theories about how to control it and how to treat offenders.

Let students know that the vocabulary associated with crime and solving crime is very specialized, but that they are given a great deal of help with this vocabulary within the chapters. Furthermore, many of them will be familiar with some crime terminology from movies and TV dramas in English that they have seen.

Chapter 7

Crime and Criminals

Look at the photograph and discuss its relationship to the chapter title and the description of the chapter on the unit title page.

1 GETTING STARTED (Student's Book pages 98–100)

The introductory paragraph discusses *deviance*, a term that may give students some comprehension difficulty. Let them know that it will be explained in the first reading passage.

READING AND THINKING ABOUT THE TOPIC

Read through the passage with students, helping them pronounce any unfamiliar terms.

Answers to step 2 (Student's Book page 99)

1 Deviant behavior is unacceptable to society, but not all deviant behaviors are criminal. A *crime* is an illegal deviant behavior.

2 Categories of crime include felonies, misdemeanors, violent, nonviolent, white-collar, blue-collar, and "modern" crimes that have been made possible by technology.

3 It is difficult to know how many crimes are committed because not all crimes are reported and not all criminals are caught.

SHARING YOUR OPINION

Students are likely to have different responses to the photograph and the list of deviant behaviors. Encourage them to express their opinions openly.

BRAINSTORMING ABOUT THE TOPIC

Read through the commentary box with students.

1, 2 | After students have been working in pairs for a while, draw the word map on the board and elicit ideas about how to fill it out.

☊ BUILDING BACKGROUND KNOWLEDGE ON THE TOPIC: TECHNICAL TERMS

1 | Before students listen to the recorded material, read through the types of crime and their definitions (in the left column of the chart) with them.

Answers to step 1 (Student's Book page 100)

Type of crime	Report number
Arson (setting property on fire)	5
Burglary (going into a building to steal something)	1
Motor vehicle theft (stealing a car)	6
Murder (killing someone, also called "homicide")	7
Rape (forcing someone to have sexual relations)	3
Shoplifting (stealing from a store)	4
Weapons possession (having a weapon without a license)	2

2 | After pairs have compared answers, verify the answers as a class.

2 AMERICAN VOICES: Evelina, Arpad, Gail, and Tom

(Student's Book pages 101–105)

Read through the introductory paragraph with students. Elicit opinions about what the interviewees might say.

BEFORE THE INTERVIEWS

EXAMINING GRAPHIC MATERIAL

1 | **Answers to step 1** (Student's Book page 101)

Chart 1: Arrests by Age Group
a Over 35: 28.9%
b 25–35: 25.6%
c Under 25: 45.5%

Chart 2: Arrests by Gender
a Male: 78%
b Female: 22%

2 | Allow time for students to discuss whether any of the information is surprising and why.

INTERVIEW WITH EVELINA AND ARPAD: Crime in society today

Look at the picture of Evelina and Arpad with their son, Daniel, on page 102 of the Student's Book. Read the vocabulary items in the box on pages 101–102 aloud, allocating time for questions about meaning, use, and pronunciation of each one.

♫ ANSWERING TRUE/FALSE QUESTIONS

1 | Elicit from students why true/false questions can be tricky. If they can't respond, ask them to reread the commentary box about true/false questions on page 55 of the Student's Book and then respond. Then have students read the eight statements carefully.

2 | Make sure that students take notes and then answer the questions in step 1 based on their notes.

Answers to step 2 (Student's Book page 102)
1 True.
2 False. He says that rowdy groups of teenagers do bother him; he usually crosses to the other side of the street.
3 False. Evelina says that guns are her biggest fear about living in the city.
4 False. He says that someone was recently shot in a bookstore in the safest part of the city.
5 True.
6 True.
7 False. He says that parents, not teachers, are the main people responsible for teaching their children to avoid violence.
8 True.

INTERVIEW WITH GAIL AND TOM: *Being the victim of a crime*

Look at the pictures of Gail and Tom. Read the vocabulary items in the box aloud, allocating time for questions about meaning, use, and pronunciation of each one.

♫ RETELLING WHAT YOU HAVE HEARD

| Read through the commentary box with the students.

1 | Explain to students that the questions in this step are to give them a preview of the interview and some of its important points.

2 | Encourage students to take full notes. Tell them that their aim should be to retell what they have heard as fully as possible.

3 | It is very important that students not read from their notes when they retell what they have heard. Reading from notes defeats the purpose of the activity, which is to be able to speak about something you have heard from memory.
     After the students have worked in pairs, ask for several volunteers to retell what they have heard to the class. Since the retelling will vary from student to student, point out the differences and that there is almost always more than one way to say something.

Sample answer to step 3 (Student's Book page 104)
Gail was mugged by some young teenagers when she was walking home alone late at night. They threatened to kill her if she didn't give them all her money. She only had four dollars in her purse, but they took it. They didn't hurt her, though. Tom was robbed several times. Once, his apartment was burglarized. Another time he had his wallet stolen by a pickpocket. When his apartment was burglarized, it was ransacked and the thieves took his camera, stereo, and paperwork. He said he lost

personal things that he couldn't replace. When his wallet was stolen, he lost a letter from his girlfriend that had symbolic value for him.

Gail had mixed feelings about being mugged. She was nervous, but she also wanted to tell the kids who robbed her to go home and stop hanging out on the street. She felt that the kids really needed attention from their parents. Tom, on the other hand, felt angry and violated. He also felt helpless because there was nothing he could do.

Gail did not report the crime, but Tom did.

AFTER THE INTERVIEWS

EXAMINING GRAPHIC MATERIAL

Answers to step 2 (Student's Book page 104)

1 Motor vehicle theft and robbery get reported most frequently.

2 Rape and thefts less than $50 get reported least frequently.

3 Answers will vary. People possibly feel that there is nothing that can be done if small amounts of money are stolen. The failure to report rape might involve feelings of fear, shame, and helplessness. Car theft is more frequently reported because of the possibility of the police finding the stolen car.

4 Answers will vary. Perhaps crimes are not reported because there is little hope that the police can help.

PERSONALIZING THE TOPIC

Answers will vary and students should be encouraged to share their opinions.

3 IN YOUR OWN VOICE (Student's Book page 106)

SHARING YOUR OPINION

This activity gives students the opportunity to develop their fluency and speak about a wide range of crime-related topics. Crime can be a difficult topic to discuss, so care has been taken to include topics that are less personal, such as crime novels or movies.

Typically, the "Find someone who . . ." activity involves a great degree of student freedom. Students can choose the boxes they wish to focus on and the classmates to whom they wish to speak.

Take the opportunity to observe individual students, supply vocabulary, and make sure that everyone gets the chance to participate.

After the game is over, some or all of the questions can be reviewed in a whole class setting. Interesting topics can be developed further and used for writing practice outside of class.

4 ACADEMIC LISTENING AND NOTE TAKING: Crime and Ways of Solving Crime (Student's Book pages 107–112)

BEFORE THE LECTURE

BUILDING BACKGROUND KNOWLEDGE ON THE TOPIC: TECHNICAL TERMS

Read through the commentary box with students. This task is meant to introduce students to difficult vocabulary and show the technique of grouping new terms, which can be a useful skill when approaching new words.

You may need to supply support. Students may also wish to use their dictionaries and add words of their own to the categories.

Answers (Student's Book page 107)

Categories of crime: felony, misdemeanor, white-collar crime, blue-collar crime

Types of crime: identity theft, fare evasion, pickpocketing, kidnapping

Methods of solving crime: DNA testing, crime hotline, fingerprinting, psychological profiling

People who commit crime or are involved in punishing crime: accused, judge, jury, defendant

∩ NOTE TAKING: CLARIFYING YOUR NOTES

Read through the commentary box with students. Let them know that almost all students have questions as they listen to a lecture. It is important that they not be afraid to ask about any item that they have not understood.

Answers to step 2 (Student's Book page 108)

The correct spelling of *misdimors* is *misdemeanors*.

A misdemeanor is punished with more than 15 (not 50) days in prison, but less than one year.

The judge (not the jury) decides the punishment.

LECTURE, Part One: Types of Crime

GUESSING VOCABULARY FROM CONTEXT

Answers to step 2 (Student's Book page 109)

1 c
2 f
3 g
4 h
5 d
6 b
7 e
8 a

2 | After students listen to Part One of the lecture, check to make sure they have noted their questions with circles, question marks, or asterisks. Have students share their questions with one another and show you their lecture notes.

3 | Encourage students to help answer each other's questions.

LECTURE, Part Two: Ways of Solving Crime

GUESSING VOCABULARY FROM CONTEXT

Answers (Student's Book page 110)

1 a
2 c
3 b
4 c
5 a
6 b
7 c
8 c

🎧 **NOTE TAKING: USING YOUR NOTES TO ANSWER TEST QUESTIONS**

| Read through the commentary box with students.

1 | Take time to make sure students understand the questions.

2 | Remind students to choose a format for their notes, e.g., columns, outline, or map. Also remind students that they should take complete notes on the lecture, not just the answers to the questions in step 1.

After they have taken notes, allow time for them to organize their notes clearly in their chosen format. Offer support as necessary.

3 | Students can review their notes before answering, but make sure they do not read from their notes.

Sample answers to step 3 (Student's Book page 111)

1 Interrogation means questioning people who might have committed a crime or who might have information about a crime. It can help the police to establish many basic facts.

2 People who are afraid to give the information publicly might use this system – for example, a family member of the criminal.

3 Fingerprints are very useful in identifying criminals because everyone's fingerprints are unique.

4 Psychological profiling involves looking at the way the crime was committed and then trying to understand the personality and motivation of the person who committed it.

5 Hidden cameras are controversial because they involve issues of privacy.

6 DNA is 99% accurate.

AFTER THE LECTURE

APPLYING WHAT YOU HAVE LEARNED

It can be very interesting for students to follow a crime story in newspapers. Many stories capture the public imagination and become popular topics of discussion.

Allow students to use several articles about the same crime investigation or trial if they are available. If you wish, you can also allow them to use information about the crime investigations or trials they have chosen from radio or TV reports.

THINKING CRITICALLY ABOUT THE TOPIC

White-collar crime is a topic that is frequently in the news these days and students will probably be interested in discussing it.

Chapter 7 Lecture Quiz

See the Lecture Quiz section at the back of this manual for a photocopiable quiz on the lecture for Chapter 7. Quiz answers can be found on pages 137–141.

Chapter 8

Controlling Crime

Look at the photograph and discuss its relationship to the chapter title and the chapter description on the unit title page.

1 GETTING STARTED (Student's Book pages 113–115)

Read through the introductory paragraph with students.

READING AND THINKING ABOUT THE TOPIC

The passage presents different opinions about the best way to reduce crime. Make sure students understand the following terms: *alarmingly, controversial, discourage, tougher, stricter,* and *prison terms.*

Answers to step 2 (Student's Book page 114)

1 One approach is to stop crime from happening in the first place; another is to punish it more harshly.

2 Educational and social programs could discourage young people from committing crimes.

🎧 LISTENING FOR OPINIONS

Read through the commentary box with students. Remind them that a speaker's tone of voice is a clue to his or her degree of certainty when expressing opinions. You might model various tones of voice with the examples in the right column: "I think . . . ," "I believe . . . ," etc.

1 | Allow time for students to read the chart of types of crime and corresponding examples. Discuss any questions they may have.

2 | **Answers to step 2** (Student's Book page 115)
   1 (Assault and robbery): Sure
   2 (Abduction): Not sure
   3 (Vandalism): Sure
   4 (Delinquent payment): Not sure
   5 (Impersonation/breaking and entering): Sure
   6 (False ID): Sure

2 AMERICAN VOICES: David and Amy (Student's Book pages 116–119)

Read through the introductory paragraph with students. Make sure they understand that *juvenile crime* refers to crime committed by young people under the age of legal responsibility.

Ask for a volunteer to remind the class of the two approaches to reducing crime that were explained in the reading passage in "Reading and Thinking About the Topic" on pages 113–114 in the Student's Book.

BEFORE THE INTERVIEWS

SHARING YOUR OPINION

Encourage students to express their opinions freely and to share any anecdotes that they wish to.

INTERVIEW WITH DAVID: Preventing juvenile crime

Look at the picture of David on page 117 of the Student's Book. Read the vocabulary items in the box on pages 116–117 aloud, allocating time for questions about meaning, use, and pronunciation of each one.

⌒ LISTENING FOR SPECIFIC INFORMATION

Sample answers to step 3 (Student's Book page 117)
1 David blames both the media and the school system.
2 He says that sometimes going to school feels like going to jail. For example, in his neighborhood there are security guards and metal detectors at the entrances to the schools. David thinks that treating kids like criminals tends to make them lash out and become violent.
3 He believes that every young person is essentially good. He thinks that if they're in a violent environment they tend to become that way, but if they're put in a caring environment, their behavior will change for the better.
4 David believes that schools should organize structured activities for students. They might be instructional programs or athletic programs. He also praises Big Brother/Big Sister programs that encourage older students to help younger ones.
5 David does believe in harsh punishments. However, he stresses that preventing crime is better than punishing it.

INTERVIEW WITH AMY: The prison experience

Look at the picture of Amy on page 118 of the Student's Book. Read the vocabulary items in the box on page 117 aloud, allocating time for questions about meaning, use, and pronunciation of each one.

🎧 LISTENING FOR MAIN IDEAS

Sample answers to step 1 (Student's Book page 118)

	What Amy thinks should happen	**The present situation**
While a convicted criminal is in prison	There should be more rehabilitation programs, both educational and drug treatment programs. Inmates should get psychological help, which would reduce the number of gangs.	Many of these programs have been cut.
After a person is released from prison	Bridge programs, which provide a transition from prison to society, are good ways to provide a transition back into society by providing former inmates with housing and jobs.	There are very few of these programs.

AFTER THE INTERVIEWS

PARAPHRASING WHAT YOU HAVE HEARD

Sample answers to step 1 (Student's Book pages 118–119)

David says that the media and the schools exacerbate the problem of juvenile crime. He believes that kids are essentially good. He thinks they need more social support systems and after-school activities. He also thinks they need good role models. However, he believes that if someone does commit a crime, the punishment should be harsh, but fair.

Amy says that to deter people from committing crime, you have to talk about social factors such as whether there are enough jobs for everyone and enough social support systems. But if convicted criminals are sent to jail, we need programs to rehabilitate them, such as drug treatment programs and educational/psychological programs. Unfortunately, many of the programs that she thinks are needed have been cut.

Amy believes that one reason there are so many recidivists is because criminals have a bad experience in jail. When prisoners are released, Amy thinks they need bridge programs to help them go back into society.

EXAMINING GRAPHIC MATERIAL

Answers to step 2 (Student's Book page 119)

1 In 1985/1989, the country that had the highest incarceration rate was South Africa. The country with the lowest incarceration rate was the Netherlands.

2 In 1995, the United States had the highest incarceration rate; it had almost doubled since 1985. Japan had the lowest incarceration rate in 1995.

3 Answers will vary.

4 Answers will vary.

3 IN YOUR OWN VOICE (Student's Book page 120)

SUPPORTING YOUR OPINION

The purpose of this exercise is to help students develop and support their opinion in a well-developed way. The technique of using different kinds of support and linking them with transition words is especially useful for academic discourse and applicable to oral and written style.

Read through the commentary box with the students.

1 | **Answers to step 1** (Student's Book page 120)

1 David believes that in order to control juvenile crime, we should try to prevent it from happening. He says that to begin with, we should have more structured after-school activities for young people. We should also have Big Brother/Big Sister programs. Additionally, we need better social support systems. And, finally, we should have harsher punishments for crimes because these would act as deterrents.

2 Amy believes that it is important to try to deter potential criminals from committing crimes. But her main point is that we should have rehabilitation procedures for criminals. First of all, there should be more programs to rehabilitate convicted criminals when they are in prison. Furthermore, these programs should have a psychological as well as an educational component. Last but not least, there should be bridge programs to help released criminals enter productive, crime-free lives.

2 | If possible, assign step 2 for written homework.

3 | If step 2 has been done at home in written form, be sure that students do not read their explanations to their group members, but rather refer to their notes only when necessary.

4 | Making a master list of the supporting details is helpful as a means of showing students the varied possibilities for supporting arguments.

ACADEMIC LISTENING AND NOTE TAKING:
The Death Penalty (Student's Book pages 121–126)

Read the introductory paragraph with students. Discuss the difference between a film that is a *documentary* and a film that is *fiction*.

BEFORE THE LECTURE

EXAMINING GRAPHIC MATERIAL

Answers to step 2 (Student's Book page 121)

1 The graph shows that the number of prisoners executed was very high in the '30s and '40s. It then declined to an extremely low rate in the '70s. Since the '70s it has been increasing again. It is still too soon to tell if the slight decline since 1999 is the beginning of a new trend or just a slight decline before another increase.

2 Answers will vary.

NOTE TAKING: RECORDING NUMERICAL INFORMATION

This task gives students an opportunity to practice the skill of recording numbers within the context of a lecture. Read through the commentary box with students, answering any questions they may have.

Answers to step 2 (Student's Book page 122)

1972	**1**
1976	**2**
600	**3**
67%	**4**
two-thirds (2/3)	**5**
9	**6**
0.5	**7**
1.1	**8**

LECTURE, Part One: Arguments Against the Death Penalty

GUESSING VOCABULARY FROM CONTEXT

Answers (Student's Book pages 122–123)

1 a
2 b
3 b
4 c
5 b
6 c
7 c
8 c

🎧 NOTE TAKING: USING YOUR NOTES TO ASK QUESTIONS AND MAKE COMMENTS

By now, students should be familiar with the note-taking task itself. What they are doing for the first time here is writing questions and comments based on their notes.

Read through the commentary box with the students.

1, 2 After students have taken their notes, give them time to write their questions and comments. Make sure that each student writes at least one question and one comment.

3 You may wish to write some of the questions and comments on the board and discuss them as a class.

LECTURE, Part Two: Questions, Answers, and Comments

GUESSING VOCABULARY FROM CONTEXT

Answers to step 2 (Student's Book page 124)

1 i
2 c
3 a
4 f
5 g
6 d
7 e
8 b
9 h

🎧 NOTE TAKING: USING YOUR NOTES TO ASK QUESTIONS AND MAKE COMMENTS

Refer to the Listening Script on pages 103–104 of this manual to see the actual student comments and Mr. Stack's responses. Encourage students to compare their own questions and comments with those made by the students in the lecture.

SUMMARIZING WHAT YOU HAVE HEARD

Sample answers to step 1 (Student's Book page 125)

> The Death Penalty
> Mr. Jonathan Stack
>
> Mr. Stack said that the death penalty is the most <u>controversial</u> issue in criminal justice. He does not believe in capital punishment. His first argument was that capital punishment does not <u>deter</u> crime. Some states that practice this form of punishment also have high rates of <u>homicide</u>. Secondly, he argued that capital punishment is not fair. The majority of people sentenced to death are <u>poor males</u>. Furthermore, a higher percentage of <u>African Americans</u> are likely to be executed than whites. Finally, he pointed out that because we are human, we sometimes <u>make mistakes</u>. He gave an example from the state of Illinois, where <u>people on death row were recently released because new evidence proved they were innocent</u>. He concluded by arguing that killing someone is <u>not in the domain of the state</u>.
>
> Five students responded to Stack. One of them pointed out that most Americans favor the death penalty in cases of murder. Stack explained that in his view, that opinion reflected <u>people's concern about violent crime in general</u>. Another student said that if people committed bad crimes, they deserved <u>to be punished</u>. Stack responded that the desire for revenge was a natural emotion but that laws were designed to <u>allow us to rise above our personal, emotional response</u>. He also said that if the death penalty were applied equally to all criminals, there would be about <u>50,000 executions</u> a year, and that would be absurd.

THINKING CRITICALLY ABOUT THE TOPIC

1 | **Answers to step 1** (Student's Book page 126)
  1 The most effective way to reduce violent crime, according to the police chiefs, is to reduce drug abuse. The least effective way of reducing violent crime, in their opinion, is to expand the death penalty.
  2 Answers will vary.

2 | You might want to review the arguments presented for and against the death penalty as a class before students discuss them in groups. Answers to step 2 will vary.

Chapter 8 Lecture Quiz

See the Lecture Quiz section at the back of this manual for a photocopiable quiz on the lecture for Chapter 8. Quiz answers can be found on pages 137–141.

Additional Ideas for Unit 4

Some key topics in this unit include crime and deviance, categories of crime, public feeling about crime, new and old ways of solving crime, ways to prevent crime, and punishments for crime, including the death penalty.

1 With your students, watch a movie about crime, prevention, and punishment. Some movies that deal with these themes are *O Brother, Where Art Thou?*, *The Shawshank Redemption*, and *Life*.

2 Have students conduct informal out-of-class interviews on people's experience with and/or feelings about crime. Students should report back to the class the stories that they are told. Alternatively, visit a youth center and conduct interviews about ways that crime can be prevented.

3 Scan the newspapers for stories about crime. Many newspapers have a "Daily Blotter" section that reports on crime in the neighborhood. Discuss prevention and punishment issues in relation to the crimes reported in the newspapers.

4 Have students share stories about the way crime is dealt with in their communities or countries.

5 Do on-line research about a particular kind of crime, such as white-collar crime or youth crime, and share the results of the research with the class.

Unit 5

Changing Societies

Unit Title Page (Student's Book page 127)

Read the title of the unit aloud and elicit ideas from students about how societies are changing. Look at the photograph and discuss its relationship to the unit title.

Read the unit summary paragraph with students. Make sure students understand these key terms: *job market* and *increased tendency*. Chapter 9 concerns how computers and the Internet have changed our world, both in our personal and professional lives. Chapter 10 deals with another big change in the contemporary world, which is the increase in the number and size of urban environments.

Cultural Change

Look at the photograph and discuss its relationship to the chapter title and the chapter description on the unit title page.

1 GETTING STARTED (Student's Book pages 128–129)

Read through the introductory paragraph with students.

READING AND THINKING ABOUT THE TOPIC

The reading passage notes a number of recent technological innovations and discusses the impact of technology on society. Students will probably know the computer-related vocabulary. Elicit definitions from them for *computerized robot, download, burn CDs,* and *digital photography.* In the second paragraph, make sure they understand *embraced, celebrated,* and *supposed benefits.*

Answers to step 2 (Student's Book page 129)

1 Surgeons in one location now use computerized robots to perform operations in another location, individuals can download music and burn their own CDs, and someone with a digital camera and access to the Internet can transmit photos to another part of the world.

2 Technology can save time and effort.

3 Some people are concerned that technology is assuming too much importance in our lives and may be having a negative effect on the way we interact with each other.

RECORDING NUMERICAL INFORMATION

1 | Preview the mini-history of the computer with students and review the way that years are expressed in English. Allow time for partners to discuss and write their guesses. You may want to open up the discussion to the class.

2 | Read the instructions with students. Explain that the word *date* can be used to mean a year, a month, and a day or to mean simply a year. In this task, they will only hear the year.

Answers to step 2 (Student's Book page 129)
   1 (500 B.C. – the answer is in the Student's Book)
   2 1642
   3 1938
   4 1956
   5 1960
   6 1968
   7 1975
   8 1985
   9 1997
  10 1997

2 AMERICAN VOICES: Nina and Kelly (Student's Book pages 130–133)

Read through the introductory paragraph with students. Elicit their thoughts on how Nina's and Kelly's opinions might be similar or different.

BEFORE THE INTERVIEWS

BUILDING BACKGROUND KNOWLEDGE ON THE TOPIC

| Read through the commentary box with the students.

1, 2 | Let students read the poem silently and discuss the meaning of *blessing* and *curse* with a partner. Then ask one or two students to read the poem aloud. Clarify any vocabulary that they do not know. Point out that the phrase "blessing or curse" suggests the mixed feelings about technology that many people have.

3 | After students have practiced with a partner, have several students present their paraphrases to the class.

INTERVIEW WITH NINA: Concerns about computers and the Internet

Look at the picture of Nina on page 131 of the Student's Book. Read the vocabulary items in the box aloud, allocating time for questions about meaning, use, and pronunciation of each one.

⌒ LISTENING FOR OPINIONS

Read through the commentary box with students. Discuss and model the tone and intonation that people might use when saying the transitional phrases.

1 Read through the instructions with students. Then elicit guesses about which alternative view Nina might present in concluding each sentence. If time permits, you could write some of the guesses on the board and compare them with what Nina actually says after students have heard the interview.

2 After students have heard the interview and compared their answers with a partner, discuss how what Nina says compares to what you wrote on the board in step 1. (Refer to the Listening Script on pages 115–116 of this manual for the content of Nina's interview.) Students don't have to use Nina's exact words, but they should correctly express her ideas.

INTERVIEW WITH KELLY: The benefits of computers and the Internet

Look at the picture of Kelly on page 132 of the Student's Book. Read the vocabulary items in the box aloud, allocating time for questions about meaning, use, and pronunciation of each one.

⌒ ANSWERING TRUE/FALSE QUESTIONS

Read the statements and brainstorm Kelly's responses with students.

Answers to step 2 (Student's Book page 133)
1 False. She is not particularly good at computers, compared to some of her friends.
2 True.
3 True.
4 False. She thinks that the phone is better for more extended interaction.
5 True.
6 False. She spends a lot of time talking to her friends online.
7 True.
8 True.

AFTER THE INTERVIEWS

EXAMINING GRAPHIC MATERIAL

Sample answers to step 1 (Student's Book page 133)
• Compared with Hispanic Americans, Whites have more Internet access.
• Between 1998 and 2000, Asian Americans' ownership of computers increased more than Whites', African Americans', and Hispanic Americans'.
• On average, Hispanic Americans own fewer computers than Whites.
• Internet access is higher among Whites than African Americans.

3 IN YOUR OWN VOICE (Student's Book page 134)

Read through the introductory paragraph with students.

SHARING YOUR OPINION

1 | The topic of language use online is likely to provoke very different reactions. Younger students or those familiar with on-line discussions are likely to find it easy to "translate" Sid and Charlene's discussion into standard English, but some students might not have seen this form of discourse before.

2 | There are no right answers for the Agree/Disagree statements. Students should feel free to express their opinions and disagree with each other's responses.

3 | Work together with the whole class to assemble a master list of "do's and don'ts" of netiquette. You could also ask the students to show the list to people outside the class and get their responses.

4 ACADEMIC LISTENING AND NOTE TAKING: Basic Work Skills Necessary in the Twenty-first Century (Student's Book pages 135–139)

Read through the introductory paragraph with the students. Make sure they understand *career counseling office*.

BEFORE THE LECTURE

PERSONALIZING THE TOPIC

After students have completed the second step of this task, ask several students who chose an older relative or friend and several who chose younger ones to explain the results of their grades.

NOTE TAKING: LISTENING FOR STRESS AND INTONATION

Read through the commentary box with students. Model the three sentence patterns. Give students time to practice the patterns in pairs. Then have one or two volunteers read each sentence aloud.

Preview the questions in step 1 and discuss where the intonation might rise and fall and which words might be stressed.

Answers to step 2 (Student's Book page 136)

1 Well, what are the skills that you need?

2 Then you decided where you were going to apply,

   put your résumé with a cover letter in a stamped envelop,

   and waited anxiously for someone to get back to you.

3 In fact, technology has not so much CHANGED the process as ENHANCED it.

4 You can research employment not just in your city, but also in your state, your region, your country, and even in other countries.

5 In addition to using newspapers and the phone, the INTERNET has become the TOOL OF PREFERENCE for getting more details on job openings, applications, and other necessary information.

LECTURE, Part One: Looking for and Applying for a Job

GUESSING VOCABULARY FROM CONTEXT

Answers to step 2 (Student's Book page 137)

1 a
2 b
3 g
4 c
5 f
6 e
7 h
8 d

🎧 NOTE TAKING: LISTENING FOR STRESS AND INTONATION

Circulate among students as they are reviewing putting their notes into a well-organized format, providing help as necessary. (Refer to the Listening Script on pages 117–119 of this manual for the content of Mr. Matos's lecture.)

Elicit from the class the content of Part One of the lecture, which they should be able to reconstruct from their notes.

LECTURE, Part Two: Getting and Keeping a Job

GUESSING VOCABULARY FROM CONTEXT

Answers to step 2 (Student's Book page 138)

1 h
2 c
3 b
4 f
5 e
6 g
7 d
8 a

Sample answers to step 3 (Student's Book page 138)

1 An applicant must be able to participate well in an interview to show that he can express himself well with clients and colleagues.

2 The basic computer skills expected in an office environment today are writing professional-looking letters, putting together Microsoft PowerPoint presentations, and organizing spreadsheets.

3 In the past, information was stored in paper calendars, rolodexes, and file cabinets, but now it is commonly stored on computers.

4 To improve your skills, you can practice on the computer in your free time and/or attend classes.

AFTER THE LECTURE

SUMMARIZING WHAT YOU HAVE HEARD

Remind students of the importance of being able to summarize well. Remind them, too, that summaries use their own words, so each student will have a slightly different paragraph. Make sure that students' summaries include both parts of the lecture.

You might want to photocopy a few of the better summaries and distribute them so that students can see how summaries vary.

Sample answer (Student's Book page 139)

Matos said that the skills a job applicant needs today include the *traditional skills* that have always been important, but also some familiarity with *technology*. You can *research* information about jobs online and you can even *apply* for a position online. At the job *interview,* applicants should show that they can express themselves well and interact with people in high-pressure situations. In order to *acquire* the *computer* skills you need, Matos recommends that you practice on the computer in your free time and attend classes.

APPLYING WHAT YOU HAVE LEARNED

Give students the opportunity to have fun with the cartoons and to use their own ideas.

SHARING YOUR OPINION

After students have discussed the questions in groups, open the discussion to the class. Make a master list on the board of the three most important qualities in an employee. List the skills students think will be most needed in the year 2050.

Chapter 9 Lecture Quiz

See the Lecture Quiz section at the back of this manual for a photocopiable quiz on the lecture for Chapter 9. Quiz answers can be found on pages 137–141.

Global Issues

Look at the photograph and discuss its relationship to the chapter title and the chapter description on the unit title page.

1 GETTING STARTED (Student's Book pages 140–142)

Read through the introductory paragraph with the students.

READING AND THINKING ABOUT THE TOPIC

Read through the passage with students. Be sure they understand the terms *urban, rural,* and *suburban.*

Answers to step 2 (Student's Book page 141)
1 One century ago, 86% of the world still lived in rural areas, but today 50% live in cities, and it is estimated that this number will soon reach 60%.
2 People move to cities in search of better jobs, better education, and more lifestyle choices.
3 Problems in cities include homelessness, environmental pollution, crime, and noise.

EXAMINING GRAPHIC MATERIAL

Answers (Student's Book page 141)
1 The approximate world population today is almost 9.5 billion people.
2 Sample answer: The world population will probably continue to increase dramatically and be at least 10 billion in 2050.
3 Answers will vary.

Read through the commentary box with students. Discuss the meaning of *sensory impressions*. Elicit from students what the five senses are: sight, sound, taste, touch, and smell.

1 | Tell students to imagine three specific places, not just general "city," etc. In this way, they will see that not all places in each of the three environments necessarily have the same sights and sounds.

2 | **Answers to items in the left column of the chart** (Student's Book page 142)

    1 Birds singing
    2 Car horn honking
    3 Subway
    4 Music from a boom box
    5 Heavy traffic
    6 Shopping mall
    7 Bubbling brook
    8 Musical concert in a concert hall
    9 People arguing over a parking spot
    10 Dogs barking

3 | Answers will vary. There are no right or wrong answers. The important thing is that students be able to explain the specific situations in which the sounds occur and why they make them feel a particular way.

4 | If time permits, allow students to share their answers with the class after they have worked with partners. Encourage them to explain the reasons for their answers.

2 AMERICAN VOICES: Barbara and Kenny (Student's Book pages 143–146)

Read through the introductory paragraph with students. Discuss the different meanings of the word *environment* when it is appears in *urban environment* and when it appears in *environmental consultant*.

BEFORE THE INTERVIEWS

SHARING YOUR OPINION

Answers may vary. People prefer different living styles and their answers will reflect their opinions. Ask students to explain their opinions with examples that make their points clear.

INTERVIEW WITH BARBARA: Life in the city, country, and suburbs

Look at the picture of Barbara on page 144 of the Student's Book. Read the vocabulary items in the box aloud, allocating time for questions about meaning, use, and pronunciation of each one.

RETELLING WHAT YOU HAVE HEARD

Read through the questions in step 1 with students. Advise them that when they retell what they have heard (in step 3), they should use the questions in step 1 only as a guide. Furthermore, they do not have to include answers to the questions in the order they appear. Encourage students to retell what they have heard in a logical way that makes sense to them, even if it doesn't follow the exact order of what Barbara says in the interview.

Sample answers to the questions in step 1 (Student's Book page 144)

1 Barbara enjoys the interactive social life. She likes to get together with her friends and relax. She also likes museums, movies, and coffee shops, which she can easily find in an urban environment.

2 When city people go to the country, they tend to get bored unless they like to putter around and build things. There is not enough to do. They are used to the fast pace of the city.

3 In the country, you need to drive everywhere, even just to buy the basic necessities.

4 Some people like the suburbs because they can hear birds and they can barbecue, but Barbara doesn't think there is anything good about the suburbs. People are dependent on cars, just as they are in the country, and no one walks in the street. Also, young people in the surburbs often have problems with drugs and alcohol.

5 Barbara doesn't think the city is lonely or dangerous. She really likes the urban lifestyle.

INTERVIEW WITH KENNY: Pros and cons of city living

Look at the picture of Kenny on page 145 of the Student's Book. Read the vocabulary items in the box on pages 144–145 aloud, allocating time for questions about meaning, use, and pronunciation of each one.

LISTENING FOR DETAILS

Remind students that it is a good idea to preview the questions before they listen to the interview. This will give them an idea of the interview's content and will allow them to make sure they understand the vocabulary.

Answers to step 2 (Student's Book page 145)

1 c
2 b
3 a
4 c
5 a
6 b
7 b
8 b
9 b

DRAWING INFERENCES

Inferential activities are challenging because they require an abstract level of thinking that asks you to draw on what you know and apply this knowledge to a different situation. Remind students that they might have different answers and that they should explain what they think based on the information that they know.

SHARING YOUR OPINION

In some ways, this activity is an extension of the inferential work the students did in the previous task. They will probably have widely varying answers to both questions. Allow sufficient time for them to think about the cartoon and then discuss it.

3 IN YOUR OWN VOICE (Student's Book pages 147–148)

MAKING A QUESTIONNAIRE TO USE IN A SURVEY

Although it might seem simple, it can be very complex to make a good questionnaire. Insist that students write down their ideas and practice asking and responding to the questions with each other. Stress the importance of writing questions that elicit answers that can easily be counted, as well as additional information that will enrich the survey.

CONDUCTING A SURVEY

Have students practice asking the questions in class before going out of class to interview other people. Once students have completed their surveys, analyzed their results, and reported them to the class, make a master list of the factors that are judged most important and allow time for the class to discuss it.

4 ACADEMIC LISTENING AND NOTE TAKING: Our Changing Cities (Student's Book pages 149–155)

Read through the introductory paragraph with students.

BEFORE THE LECTURE

BUILDING BACKGROUND KNOWLEDGE ON THE TOPIC

Be sure that students work in groups so that they do not feel embarrassed if they don't know some of the answers. Encourage them to have fun with the quiz. You could suggest that one student in each group look at the answers on page 150 of the Student's Book and let the others keep guessing for each item until they get it right.

STUDYING HANDOUTS

Read through the commentary box with students. Discuss the importance of previewing a handout. Stress the fact that handouts are not substitutes for the lecture, but are often used for purposes of illustration.

1 | Look at Handout 1 on page 150 and have students highlight vocabulary and ideas that they understand. Then help them with vocabulary they do not understand.

If time permits, you may want to use this occasion to discuss how all languages change over time. Elicit from students words or expressions in their native languages that are no longer used and words or expressions that have entered the languages recently.

It does not matter if students do not understand every term, but they should understand the basic idea that different living environments have different benefits and disadvantages. You should also discuss the meaning of *magnet*.

Answers to item 2 (Student's Book page 149)

a "Town" corresponds to "city."
"Country" corresponds to "country."
"Town-Country" corresponds to "suburbs."

b Howard's model shows "Town-Country" (suburbs) as having the most advantages. Discuss with students the fact that at the time Howard constructed his model there were no suburbs as we know them today. Howard seems to be suggesting that suburbs would become the ideal combination of the best of both city and country. The purpose of this question is for students to think about whether the suburbs have turned out to be such an ideal place.

c Answers will vary.

2 | Handout 2 also includes a lot of terms that are useful, but not vital, for understanding the content of the lecture. Help students with the vocabulary as needed. The visual models are easy to comprehend.

∩ NOTE TAKING: USING HANDOUTS TO HELP YOU TAKE NOTES

Remind students that they have already practiced writing questions and comments on their own notes in Chapters 7 and 8. In this chapter, they will practice an auxiliary skill: annotating handouts. Read through the commentary box with students.

Make sure that students understand that marking handouts is not a substitute for taking notes on their own paper about the lecture. The task requires them to circle parts of the handout *and* take notes on their own paper about what the lecturer says.

LECTURE, Part One: Reasons People Move to Cities

GUESSING VOCABULARY FROM CONTEXT

Answers to step 2 (Student's Book page 152)

1 c
2 d
3 f
4 a
5 b
6 g
7 e

🎧 NOTE TAKING: COMBINING THE SKILLS

Read through the commentary box, which is a review of the note-taking skills that students have studied and practiced.

1 | Encourage students to use as many of the skills as possible.

2 | Allow students time to revise and organize their notes. Make sure they follow up this process by analyzing their note-taking skills. You might ask them to make a list of the skills they employed in taking notes on Part One of the lecture.

3 | Make sure students have time to compare their notes and share questions and comments with a partner.

LECTURE, Part Two: Changes in the City

GUESSING VOCABULARY FROM CONTEXT

Answers to step 2 (Student's Book page 153)

1 f
2 b
3 e
4 c
5 d
6 a

🎧 NOTE TAKING: COMBINING THE SKILLS

This task requires students to analyze a partner's notes. They have been doing this informally throughout the book. In this situation, however, they are asked to do it more formally as a final review.

AFTER THE LECTURE

SUMMARIZING WHAT YOU HAVE HEARD

Remind students that in summarizing they should select the main points of the lecture and rewrite them in their own words. Their paragraphs might be quite different from the one below.

Our Changing Cities

Professor Bryan Gilroy

Many more people are moving to cities today than in the past. There are various reasons for this, some of which are shown in the handout from Ebenezer Howard's book. The main reason that many people prefer to live in a city is because there are more jobs and more opportunities to earn money in urban environments. A second reason is that cities offers comfort and convenience. There are better transportation networks, shops, and places of entertainment, as well as better educational opportunities.

As more people move to urban areas, some cities are turning into megacities (cities with more than 10 million people). Cities are growing larger and taller and urban sprawl is becoming a problem in some places. But cities are also breaking up into smaller communities. These communities are usually based on ethnic group or income level.

In the future, cities will continue to grow. We have to face the problems that they present, such as overcrowding and poverty.

GIVING GROUP PRESENTATIONS

Students have practiced this task before, in Chapter 5. If necessary, review the guidelines on page 73 of the Student's Book.

Be sure that students choose different cities, if possible, in order to make the presentations more interesting. Encourage students to be imaginative and have fun with this task.

Chapter 10 Lecture Quiz

See the Lecture Quiz section at the back of this manual for a photocopiable quiz on the lecture for Chapter 10. Quiz answers can be found on pages 137–141.

Additional Ideas for Unit 5

Some key topics in this unit include technology's impact on our lives, benefits and drawbacks of computer use, the way computers are affecting employment, the movement to cities, pros and cons of different living environments, and changes in cities.

1 With your students, watch a movie about the impact of computer technology. Some movies that deal with this theme are *The Matrix, Artificial Intelligence,* and *Antitrust.*

2 Have students conduct informal out-of-class interviews with people of different ages about their use of computers and the Internet. Alternatively, have students share their computer knowledge with each other by assigning short Internet projects, PowerPoint presentations, or reviews of new software applications.

3 With the class, read an essay or short story about technological change or lifestyle changes. Some possibilities are for technology: "Computers and the Pursuit of Happiness" by David Gelernter, or "E-mail: The Future of the Family Feud" by Candy Schulman; and for city living: "A Nice Place to Visit" by Russell Baker or "Maintaining the Crime Supply" by Barbara Ehrenreich.

4 Have students work in pairs to "visit" different cities online. Ask them to share their impressions of these cities with other students. Alternatively, have students discuss how their city has changed in their lifetime or the lifetime of their parents.

5 Have the class share photographs of different cities they have visited.

Listening Script

Listening Script

Narrator: *Academic Listening Encounters: Life in Society*
Listening, Note Taking, and Discussion
by Kim Sanabria.
Series editor: Bernard Seal.
Published by Cambridge University Press.
These CDs [Cassettes] contain the listening material for the *Academic Listening Encounters: Life in Society* Student's Book. This recording is copyright.

Narrator: CD [Cassette] 1.
Chapter 1, Marriage, Family, and the Home
Page 3
Listening for numerical information, Step 2

Narrator: One.

Man: Most adults in the United States get married, but many get divorced. The U.S. divorce rate is rising. About fifty percent of all U.S. marriages will end in divorce.

Narrator: Two.

Woman: About half of all children in the United States spend some time in a single-parent family.

Narrator: Three.

Man: The average size of an American family today is about three people – some studies say that it might be even smaller.

Narrator: Four.

Woman: There are also many "alternative" family arrangements today. For example, more than fifty percent of young couples live together before they get married.

Narrator: Five.

Man: Today, about one in ten households consists of only one person.

Narrator: Now complete the steps in your book.

Narrator: **Chapter 1, Marriage, Family, and the Home**
Page 5
Listening for details, Step 2

Interviewer: Hello, Robert. I'd like to talk to you about your family.

Robert: Well, probably the most important influence in my life was my family. Not just my mother and father, but my extended family. I grew up very close to them. I never really sought people out besides my family. And we lived together in a three-generation house.

Interviewer: Three generations in one house?

Robert: Yes, we . . . we all lived together in a big house. My mother had never in her whole life lived without her parents.

Interviewer: Wow! That is amazing!

Robert: Well, my house had my grandparents – my grandfather was still working, he wasn't retired – my grandmother, my mother, and my father. I remember feeling when I was in the car, and we were going someplace, I used to feel sorry for all the other children on the street, because they weren't going anywhere with their own families. So, I was very happy.

Interviewer: Weren't there ever any problems . . . ah . . . with you all living in the same house?

Robert: Well, there was a time – when I was in college – and, you see, my father always wanted his children with him. He was actually more protective of us than my mother was, and I remember I had a big project to do for school and they were going away for the weekend and I had decided that I wasn't going to go because I needed to do my work. And this caused a terrible problem. And I did end up going because my father was so upset. So I think, of course, as I got older I started to realize that I had to live my own life, but it wasn't that easy.

Interviewer: How many children were there?

Robert: Well, I was the oldest of three boys. And, of course, since my grandparents lived in the house, my cousins, and my aunt and uncle came to the house, and we used to dance and roller-skate in the basement and play together. I didn't play with children on my block very much.

Interviewer: It sounds like you had a really good upbringing.

Robert: Well, I have very positive feelings about my family, and the most positive feeling is love. What I learned from different people in my family are perhaps some of my best traits. My father was a very generous person, and I learned that you should care about other people. And my grandparents and parents shared the same values.

Interviewer: Well, Robert, when you look around today and see that there's more divorce, more single-parent families – what do you think?

Robert: I think that many things have changed in society today. I mean the whole world has changed and the definition of family has changed. I think that families are not necessarily blood relations. But it's important to belong to some kind of unit where people care about you and love you.

Narrator: Now complete the steps in your book.

Narrator: Chapter 1, Marriage, Family, and the Home
Page 7
Paraphrasing what you have heard, Step 2

Interviewer: Carlos, I know you grew up in a single-parent household. Can you tell me about your family?

Carlos: OK. My mother and father migrated to the U.S. from Puerto Rico when I was five-years-old and my sister was three, but then my mother left my father, so it was just my mother, my sister, and myself. And my mother was a garment worker. You know, sewing. But that industry is seasonal, so when there was work, she worked a lot. Then she would find people to take care of us until she got home. When we were a little older, we pretty much took care of ourselves.

Interviewer: Did you play with other kids in the neighborhood much?

Carlos: Oh, yeah. There was a good stretch when I was in junior high school and played out in the street a lot. After school I'd be out and just play stickball, marbles, yo-yos, and just run around the neighborhood.

Interviewer: What kind of lessons do you think you learned from your mother?

Carlos: Well, I guess there were two things. The first thing I remember is being taught to pretty much take care of myself. You know, picking up after myself around the house. And I remember her teaching me cooking, cleaning, and ironing, and I remember running errands because at dinner time, there was always something she'd forgotten to get.

Interviewer: You said you learned *two* lessons.

Carlos: I guess the other lesson was just, you know, how important it is to get an education. I remember she wanted us to learn Spanish, so she bought a blackboard and started teaching us in the house.

Interviewer: Well, Carlos, over the past generation or so, family structure has changed a lot. How important do you think these changes are?

Carlos: Well, I don't really know if it has changed that much. Sure, there's been an increase in single-parent households. But I don't know if the *family* has really changed. Who are you talking about? Rich people? Poor women have always had to work outside the house – that hasn't changed too much! But what I do think is important is having a person in the family who does what has to be done to show you the right way, so that you can get an education, moral instruction, religious outlook – some positive influence in your life, an anchor in your life. So for example, school was very influential in my life. There were enough good teachers to really point me in the right direction. It's not just what you get in the home, but other positive influences as well.

Narrator: Now complete the steps in your book.

Narrator: Chapter 1, Marriage, Family, and the Home
Page 11
Note taking: Listening for main ideas and supporting details, Step 1

Narrator: One.

Beth Handman: First, then, let's discuss rewards. A reward can be defined as a positive reinforcement for good behavior.

Narrator: Two.

Beth Handman: Punishments are the second important way in which a child is socialized. All of us have probably been punished in our lives. For example, maybe our parents stopped us from going out with friends because we did something we were not supposed to do.

Narrator: Three

Beth Handman: Parents can set a good example by showing children the kind of behavior they expect. Let me give you a personal example. I know a boy called Peter, who told me he liked to study because his mother studied with him.

Narrator: Four

Beth Handman: There's an old saying in English: "Don't do as I do. Do as I tell you." But this advice doesn't work most of the time. Some studies have suggested that if you smoke yourself, it's probably ineffective to tell a child not to smoke.

Narrator: Five.

Beth Handman: So, understandably, parents are often worried about the negative lessons that children can learn – for example, from other children, or from TV. TV can send children a lot of negative messages. In fact, it's been estimated that on average, eighty percent of programs contain violent behavior.

Narrator: Now complete the steps in your book.

Narrator: Chapter 1, Marriage, Family, and the Home
Page 13
Note taking: Organizing your notes in columns, Step 2

Beth Handman: Hi. Welcome. Today we're going to be talking about how children learn social behaviors, especially how they learn lessons from the family – the most basic unit of our social structure.

There's a lot of discussion these days about how families are changing and whether non-traditional families have a good or bad effect on children. But it's important to remember that the type of family a child comes from is not nearly as important as the kind of love and support that exist in the home.

I'd like to focus on three of the ways that children acquire their behavior: through rewards, punishments, and finally, modeling. First, then, let's discuss rewards. A reward can be defined as a positive reinforcement for good behavior. An example of a reward is when a parent says: "If you eat your vegetables, you can have ice cream for dessert." Or a parent might say: "Finish your homework first. Then you can watch TV." Most parents use rewards unconsciously, because they want their children to behave well. For example, a parent might give a gift to a child because the child behaved well. Or parents might give a child money for doing what the parents asked.

The opposite of a reward is a punishment. Punishments are the second important way in which a child is socialized. All of us have probably been punished in our lives. For example, maybe our parents stopped us from going out with friends because we did something we were not supposed to do. Or maybe they wouldn't let us watch TV because we got a bad grade on a test.

Both rewards and punishments are controversial. Many people think they are not effective or necessary, especially when used often. Let's take this situation: A young boy has been asked to take out the garbage. Listen to Situation A: The parent says: "If you take out the garbage for me, I'll give you a cookie." Some people argue that this reward is unnecessary because it's like a bribe. They argue that the child should be taught that it's his duty to help with household chores, and that he should not get a special reward for doing something that's his responsibility. Situation B would go something like this: "Justin, please take out the trash now." And Justin says: "OK, Dad."

Not surprisingly, punishment is extremely controversial, especially when the punishment is physical. Some of us grew up expecting to be spanked if we misbehaved. For example, our parents may have hit us on the hand if we talked back to them. But I don't agree that spanking can teach children anything, and sadly, some children are subject to really serious physical abuse. According to a study I just read, one in twenty-two children is a victim of physical abuse. Children who come from homes where violence is used to solve problems are much more likely to abuse their own children when they become adults and have their own families.

Narrator: Now complete the steps in your book.

Narrator: Chapter 1, Marriage, Family, and the Home
Page 15
Note taking: Organizing your notes in columns, Step 2

Beth Handman: The third way that children are taught how to act is through modeling. Modeling means that they learn to behave by following an example. Modeling is probably the most powerful way that children learn social skills. Children look for role models in their life, meaning people who they admire and want to copy. Children's first role models are their parents. Parents can teach children by modeling appropriate behavior, as various researchers have noted. Parents can set a good example by showing children the kind of behavior they expect. Let me give you a personal example. I know a boy called Peter who told me he liked to study because his mother studied with him. This is an important lesson that he learned just by copying his mother's behavior.

There's an old saying in English: "Don't do as I do. Do as I tell you." If you say that to a child, it means that the child should *not* copy what you do, but instead, just do what you are telling the child to do. But this advice doesn't work most of the time. Some studies have suggested that if you smoke yourself, it's probably ineffective to tell a child not to smoke. The child will most likely think: "Well, my mother smokes, so why shouldn't I?"

Modeling is the most important way that children learn. And of course, parents are not the only people teaching children. Other family members and friends are also models. Many people do not even realize the impact they can have on a child that they know, but children carefully watch other people around them and notice the way they behave. It's important to note here that it is common for babysitters, relatives, and childcare centers to take care of children, as well as parents. So children are exposed to many models of behavior. They learn from each other, from their teachers, and from society itself. So, understandably, parents are often worried about the negative lessons that children can learn – for example, from other children, or from TV. TV can send children a lot of negative messages. In fact, it's been estimated that, on average, eighty percent of programs contain violent behavior.

I'd like to conclude by reminding you, again, that the most important thing for children is to grow up in an environment where there are fair rules that are clearly established and followed consistently by everyone. If the child knows what the expectations are, he or she will find it much easier to acquire "good behavior." And if the child is loved and exposed to strong, positive role models, the child will quickly begin to grow in a healthy way.

Narrator: Now complete the steps in your book.

2

Narrator: Chapter 2: The Power of the Group Page 18
Listening for specific information, Step 2

Interviewer: Would you go to the wedding, Rebecca?

Rebecca: Of course I would! If it's your family, you're kind of expected to go along, aren't you?

Jim: I disagree. I wouldn't go. I'd say I had to work that weekend, or make some excuse like that!

Interviewer: OK, Jim. Would you go to the movie with your friends?

Jim: Yeah, sure. It might be good! Reviews aren't always right!

Rebecca: I'd go too. I agree, sometimes the newspaper says that a movie's no good, but it turns out you like it. And even if it's bad, I'll have a good time with my friends, anyway.

Interviewer: And the shoes? Rebecca, would you consider buying them?

Rebecca: Well, maybe not buying them, but I might try them on. They might look good on me! And if everyone's wearing them, perhaps they're really comfortable or something.

Jim: No way. I don't care what my friends think. Fashion is a personal choice!

Interviewer: All right, last question. Would you go away with your parents?

Jim: Definitely not! I really don't want to spend the whole weekend with my parents' friends, especially if I have to study.

Rebecca: Me neither! My mom would probably put pressure on me to go. She'd tell me that I could do my work in the country. But I

wouldn't want to spend a weekend with their friends, either.

Narrator: Now complete the steps in your book.

Narrator: Chapter 2: The Power of the Group Page 20
Listening for main ideas, Step 2

Interviewer: Henry, they say that adolescence is the time when people begin to get most pressure from their peers. Do you think that's true?

Henry: What I've seen is that adolescence is the time when the pressure begins to shift from the family and the school to friends. I think it begins about eleven, but comes into full bloom at about thirteen, fourteen.

Interviewer: What actually happens then?

Henry: Well the first thing you see is that adolescents begin to make fashion statements. And certainly those ideas don't come from you. You can tell at a glance that they don't come from you! Like wearing baggy pants that look like they're falling down, and, you know, piercing their ears. My younger son began to ask if he could dye his hair blue.

Interviewer: And what did you say?

Henry: We said when he was a little older he could make that decision, with the hope that that fad would have passed out of style.

Interviewer: OK, but where would you draw the line? I mean, you'd let him wear baggy pants, but would you let him dye his hair?

Henry: I think, in the end, I would. But not without a fight.

Interviewer: So, what other things happen?

Henry: Well, as the kids get older you start to lose them, because they're always talking on the phone, or talking online, or doing other things. Even when they're home – they're in their room most of the time talking on the phone – and not just talking on the phone. They might be talking to one person on the phone and two other people online. And the only thing you know for sure is they're not talking to you!

Interviewer: Do you think this is all normal behavior? I mean, should you be trying to monitor it?

Henry: I think both. It's healthy to develop your own values, your own tastes. But I also think that parents should be monitoring it. When it's a question of fashion, that's OK. Where you draw the line is when they're doing something dangerous, or illegal – drugs, smoking, drinking.

Interviewer: Is there any advice you could give parents?

Henry: Well, one thing is to think back to your own experience as a teenager. I must say I find myself repeating the same annoying language my father used with me. I have to try to remember not to do that.

Interviewer: So how you talk to your kids is important.

Henry: Yes, and it's hard to watch your kids doing things you don't want them to do. For example, my kids are into video games, and I can't find any value whatsoever in these games. But I think that you don't have to like everything your kids do. As long as it's not dangerous or illegal.

Narrator: Now complete the steps in your book.

Narrator: Chapter 2, The Power of the Group Page 21
Listening for specific information, Step 2

Interviewer: Hey Victor, how old are you?

Victor: I'm gonna be twelve next month.

Interviewer: Well, I'm asking people about peer pressure. Y-you know who your peers are, right?

Victor: Peers?

Interviewer: Your friends, you know. People in your class.

Victor: Oh, yeah.

Interviewer: Well, do you think that they have a lot of influence on you? Like, like, for instance, do you ever change your mind about something because of what your friends say?

Victor: Well, sometimes.

Interviewer: Can you give me an example? A-a time when your friends influenced you?

Victor: Well, all my friends have this video game, and I want one, too. So I asked my Mom. But she said it's a waste of money. But my friend Marcos has one, and I really like it. So I'm gonna ask my Dad if he can get my Mom to change her mind.

Interviewer: Good luck with that, Victor! But why do you think your friends influence you?

Victor: I guess I'm just jealous, because I want a video game, too. Loads of people in my grade have that video game, so I want it.

Interviewer: So you think you want that game mostly because your friends have one?

Victor: Sure, I suppose so.

Interviewer: Thanks a lot, Victor. . . . Samira, you're a sophomore in high school right?

Samira: Uh-huh. Tenth grade.

Interviewer: And would you say that your peers – your friends and the people you hang out with – have a lot of influence on you?

Samira: Totally. I mean, we talk about everything, and, like, I have my own opinions about stuff and all that, but we always talk everything over.

Interviewer: How important is it for you to be one of the group?

Samira: Well, you don't want to be just like sheep, you know, do everything that everyone else is doing. I mean, you've got to think for yourself. You can't conform all the time. But sure, my friends influence me a lot.

Interviewer: More than your parents?

Samira: Well, probably, at this point. Yes.

Interviewer: Why do you think peers have so much influence over each other?

Samira: Well, you're in the same boat, right? I mean you share your culture. You share who you are.

Narrator: Now complete the steps in your book.

**Narrator: Chapter 2, The Power of the Group
Page 26
Note taking: Listening for organizational phrases, Step 3**

Narrator: Listen to these phrases from the lecture.

Iván Zatz: The subject of today's lecture is . . .

I'm going to focus on three main ideas in this lecture . . .

First of all, we will consider . . .

Secondly, I will describe . . .

Finally, I'll mention . . .

First, then . . .

Now let's turn to . . .

To conclude, let's look at . . .

Narrator: Now complete the steps in your book.

**Narrator: Chapter 2, The Power of the Group
Page 27
Note taking: Organizing your notes in outline form, Step 2**

Iván Zatz: The subject of today's lecture is Culture Shock – Group Pressure in Action.

Culture shock, as you know, is the term used to describe the experience many people have when they travel to another country, and it can be seen as a manifestation of group pressure in action. It is a good example of group pressure, because it shows what happens when an individual suddenly experiences different cultural rules – the rules of another cultural group.

Now culture shock is a complex phenomenon, but I'm going to focus on three main ideas in this lecture. First of all, we will consider the reasons why people experience culture shock. Secondly, I will describe the different stages of this experience. Finally, I'll mention some possible applications of this research because although you might think that culture shock affects, say, only travelers, that is not the case. In fact, cross-cultural studies have immense practical value for modern society.

First, then, why do people experience culture shock? Think about this for a minute. When you grow up in a particular set of surroundings, naturally you get used to the rules and guidelines that govern the behavior of the people around you. In a sense, you become totally dependent on the rules of your social group. You tend not to question them; you just accept them without thinking. These rules are often not clearly articulated, and therefore, you're not aware of their impact. In other words, you are not necessarily conscious of them. They only become important when, for example, you go to another country or a different environment that's governed by a different set of rules. In fact, this experience can be so shocking that it has been compared to having a bucket of cold water thrown over you. Culture shock happens precisely because you cannot use your own culture as a map to guide your own behavior and your own understanding of what surrounds you. You're totally out of control, just as if you were driving along a highway in the dark, without a road map. And because of this, people often behave irrationally. It's a highly stressful experience, and there are different symptoms in different stages.

Narrator: Now complete the steps in your book.

**Narrator: Chapter 2, The Power of the Group
Page 29
Note taking: Copying a lecturer's diagrams and charts, Step 2**

Iván Zatz: Now, let's turn to the different stages of culture shock. Most researchers agree that there are three main stages. If you were to depict it on paper, you might draw a "wave" shape, as I've done in this diagram.

The first stage, the "crest" or highest part of the wave, is often referred to as the "honeymoon" stage. It's the time when you first arrive in a new culture and are confronted with a whole set of different rules. What are the emotions that you experience during this time? Even though this is a new and often strange experience, people don't usually react with fear. Surprisingly, there is often a feeling of euphoria. The most common reactions at this time are excitement, fascination, and enthusiasm. Of course, you're on your guard because of the strangeness in the situation. But, at this stage, cultural differences are likely to seem exciting, rather than threatening.

The second stage has been called the "let down." Here are some feelings that people experience during this phase: irritation, hostility, and confusion. They might also feel exhausted, lonely and nervous. These feelings happen because travelers have to unlearn their own cultural habits and values as they spend more time in a new country and are expected to function according to the ways of that place. They may feel like lost children without protection. They probably want to go home, but if they can't do that, they spend a lot of time with other people from their own country, in order to get back a sense of safety.

The final stage is one of resignation. Even if visitors aren't completely comfortable, they do become adjusted to the new environment. Or at least, they stop feeling that they need to defend their own culture every time they encounter a habit or value they don't easily recognize. They might never recapture the honeymoon period, but they're not as depressed as they were during stage two.

To conclude, let's look at some practical applications of the research. Well, remember I mentioned that it doesn't just apply to tourists on vacation, or even international students. In our world of rapid transportation and population mobility, many societies have recent immigrants, sometimes in large numbers. This becomes a general social challenge, because immigrants are going through even more cultural shock than tourists. Furthermore, older residents of a country with large numbers of new immigrants can experience their own form of "internal culture shock" when they see neighborhoods or even larger regions where people speak a foreign language or eat unfamiliar food or behave according to cultural patterns brought from their own countries. Because cultural differences can sometimes lead to tense relationships between different ethnic groups, it is vital that people try to learn as much as possible – get some cross-cultural training if they can – about the different cultures in their own societies. Because the more we learn about our differences, the easier it is to live in a world where different cultures have to live in close contact with each other.

Narrator: Now complete the steps in your book.

3

Narrator: Chapter 3, Growing Up Male or Female
Page 34
Building background knowledge on the topic, Step 2

Narrator: One.

Woman: What are little boys made of?
Frogs and snails, and puppy dogs' tails,
That's what little boys are made of.
What are little girls made of?
Sugar and spice,
And all things nice.
That's what little girls are made of.

Narrator: Two.

Man: Jack be nimble,
Jack be quick,
Jack jump over
The candlestick.

Narrator: Three.

Woman: Polly, put the kettle on,
Polly, put the kettle on,

Polly, put the kettle on,
We'll all have tea.
Lucy, take it off again,
Lucy, take it off again,
Lucy, take it off again,
They've all gone away.

Narrator: Four.

Man: Little Miss Muffet
Sat on a tuffet,
Eating her curds and whey.
Along came a spider
And sat down beside her
And frightened Miss Muffet away.

Narrator: Five.

Woman: Georgie Porgie, pudding and pie,
Kissed the girls and made them cry;
When the boys came out to play,
Georgie Porgie ran away.

Narrator: Now complete the steps in your book.

Narrator: Chapter 3, Growing Up Male or Female
Page 36
Answering multiple-choice questions, Step 2

Interviewer: Hi, Linda. I'd like to ask you about bringing up a son in today's world

Linda: I think the most critical issue is to raise a son who's proud of being himself, who will be a good parent and a good husband. The other thing is that he should be sensitive to the issues that women have.

Interviewer: And how are boys' issues different from girls'?

Linda: Boys tend to be more competitive. They're expected to be a lot tougher, they're expected to excel in sports – and a lot of social relationships and friendships grow outta sports. So it's "who're you playing basketball with?" or "are you on the football team?" Girls tend to form groups more easily without sports.

Interviewer: You know, I read somewhere that men need to "do something" – like, like sports – to get together.

Linda: Yeah, that's true. When boys are younger, school brings them together. But later, men tend to use sports as that thing they do together. They talk about sports and there's a major bonding that goes on around sports.

Interviewer: Yeah, I-I think you're right about that.

Linda: And some people think that boys are closed emotionally, but *I* think that boys now share a lot of their intimate feelings with other boys. Of course they still tease each other very harshly and relentlessly. But they're more open about things that scare them than they were in the past.

Interviewer: What kinds of things do you think that boys are scared of?

Linda: I think they're scared of . . . not being accepted, of not being liked. Of not being intelligent enough, of not being strong enough, of not being fast enough, of not being attractive enough.

Interviewer: Do you think it's harder to bring boys up these days?

Linda: Yes. In the old days, roles were more prescribed. But there's a lot more flexibility now. You have to know how to make a role for yourself, structure yourself. You don't go into your dad's business. There's no lifetime employment anymore. It's a lot more exciting and creative and challenging, but it's also scary. It takes a lot more inner strength, I think.

Interviewer: Linda, when you look at your son, what are your dreams and hopes for him?

Linda: I want him to grow up to be a really good person. I want him to be very, very caring. To be a good husband and a good friend who understands that he is a member of society, and he has certain responsibilities toward society. And I want him to be financially stable, but not necessarily wealthy. And I'd like him to love whatever he does for a living. Because I think that's what makes a happy man, a happy father, a happy person.

Narrator: Now complete the steps in your book.

Interviewer: Shingo, were the boys and girls in your family brought up with the same rules?

Shingo: Well, I have a younger brother and sister. My sister's the youngest. And of course my parents care about me and my brother, but they *take* care of my sister more. Like, they shelter her more. For example, it was OK for me to move to the U.S. from Japan and work here. They didn't mind that I wouldn't be that close. And I like doing things by myself. I don't want to be restricted. I like the freedom.

Interviewer: And your sister?

Shingo: They just want her to stay around them, marry someone close by. When she was growing up, she never really wanted to go out. She mostly stayed in her room, or went shopping or wherever with my parents. And now she's twenty, but she still hangs out with them a lot, more than we ever did.

Interviewer: Don't your parents worry about you and your brother?

Shingo: Of course, but they feel like we're going to be OK because we've always been very independent. But my sister is always with my parents. If she goes shopping, they pay for her. Everywhere!

Interviewer: But, do you think that's because of her personality, or is it because she's a girl?

Shingo: Well, it's definitely because she's a girl that she's so shy. And, I guess, my parents just expect her to be with them longer than we were.

Interviewer: And, cooking. Did your parents teach you how to cook?

Shingo: No, but they didn't teach my sister either!

Interviewer: So who cooked in your house?

Shingo: My mother! But I learned to cook from cookbooks. When I left Japan, I had to cook for myself. And I like cooking. When we were in elementary school, everyone learned a little bit of cooking. And girls did sewing, too.

Interviewer: And what about later on?

Shingo: Well, in junior high school, the boys did woodwork and the girls carried on with cooking and sewing. But nowadays, there's less discrimination than there used to be. So in my opinion, you have to give kids choices. And if the girls want to do woodwork, we should let them. If boys want to sew, why not? Things are becoming more and more equal. Let kids do whatever they want. That's one of the most important things.

Interviewer: And it doesn't matter if they're boys or girls?

Shingo: No, it doesn't matter to me. My parents let me have a lot of freedom. I wanna do the same thing for my children. If they wanna be independent, that's OK. And if they need a lot of my support, I'll give it to them, like my parents do to my sister. You have to be flexible.

Narrator: Now complete the steps in your book.

Mary Frosch: I'm going to be discussing the benefits of single-sex education. As a teacher and advisor in an all-girls' school, I am often asked to defend single-sex education – specifically, all-girls' education – as if girls' schools were on trial. I, personally, strongly recommend single-sex education for girls. But the arguments against this form of education can be quite powerful, so I would like to begin by pointing out three of the main arguments against all-girls' schools.

Narrator: Now complete the steps in your book.

Mary Frosch: I'm going to be discussing the benefits of single-sex education. As a teacher and advisor in an all-girls' school, I am often asked to defend single-sex education – specifically, all-girls' education – as if girls' schools were on trial. I, personally, strongly recommend single-sex education for girls. But the arguments against this form of education can be quite powerful, so I would like to begin by pointing out three of the main arguments against all-girls' schools.

First of all, critics of all-girls' schools argue that the separation of the sexes seems old-fashioned. It goes against the aims and the goal of feminists and liberal educators, which is to provide fairness: to make sure boys and girls have the same educational opportunities and are treated in the same way.

Secondly, the critics say that in single-sex schools, boys and girls can't develop the ability to interact with one another. They point out that in single-sex schools, boys and girls can't learn how to be comfortable with each other and also how to compete with each other.

The third criticism is that single-sex schools don't provide children with a smooth transition into the adult world where men and women live together. In single-sex schools, these critics say, boys and girls cannot become prepared for a world in which they will work, play, and live together as adults.

But although these are serious arguments, I believe that single-sex education is beneficial for girls. In the second part of this lecture, I'll focus on two strong advantages of single-sex education: It values girls' unique qualities and it helps girls develop self-confidence.

Narrator: Now complete the steps in your book.

Mary Frosch: The first real benefit of all-girls' education is that it values girls' unique qualities – the qualities that make them different from boys. What are these unique qualities? Well, I'm going to list a few. First of all, girls can often concentrate on higher-level, abstract thinking at an earlier age than boys can. Secondly, they can often work for longer periods of time. Girls also enjoy collaborative learning activities and so they work well in groups. Finally, as girls mature, they are often kind and cooperative, rather than competitive. These four qualities are valued in all-girls' schools.

The second benefit of single-sex education is that it helps girls develop self-confidence. I strongly believe that girls become more self-confident without the distraction and different learning styles of boys. In a single-sex environment girls enjoy being leaders. They offer help to others and they also ask for help when they need it; for example, if they don't understand a math or science concept, they'll ask for clarification. But when girls are in the same classrooms as boys, they often lose their self-esteem. Boys are sometimes louder and may jump up out of their seats and wave their arms in people's faces if they know the answer to a teacher's question. If this happens, girls typically sink back in their chairs and wait for the boys to quiet down. But if there are no boys around, girls can feel free and be themselves.

Now, it's true that all-girls' schools do separate girls from the real world while they are growing up. *But,* in the "real," adult world, boys are the ones who set the rules of the game, and these rules don't necessarily reflect the needs or talents of girls. In an all-girls' school, girls can become confident enough to challenge the rules. And then, perhaps, they can change the "real" world into a place designed to accommodate both women and men.

Narrator: Now complete the steps in your book.

4

**Narrator: Chapter 4, Gender Issues Today
Page 51
Listening for specific information, Step 3**

Narrator: One: The employee is going to get married.

Jack: If the employee is a man, people think he'll work harder because he'll need to keep his job, but if the employee is a woman, people often think that she'll have a baby and leave her job.

Narrator: Two. The employee has a family picture on his or her desk.

Jack: If the employee is a man, people think "He loves his family," but if the employee is a woman, people think, "She's more interested in her husband and her children than she is in her career."

Narrator: Three. The employee is talking with a co-worker.

Jack: If the employee is a man people think they're talking about something important, but if the employee is a woman, people usually think they're just chatting.

Narrator: Four. The employee is going to go on a business trip.

Jack: If the employee is a man people think the trip will be good for his career, but if the employee is a woman, they say, "What will her husband think?"

Narrator: Now complete the steps in your book.

**Narrator: Chapter 4, Gender Issues Today
Page 54
Answering multiple-choice questions, Step 2**

Interviewer: Belinda, do you think you've ever been discriminated against because you're a woman?

Belinda: Well, let's see, I have two answers for that. The first answer is yes – that's my gut feeling. But sometimes I think no, I'm not being discriminated against. I just need to try harder. I guess I'm saying yes and no. Look, we're in a society where yes, discrimination is definitely going on in the business world. I see women getting paid less than men do, for the same position. And often women get jobs as assistants – but they're the ones who do all the work! Also there's this "old boys' club," the support network that men have. Men do help each other, and they could help women, too. But they don't.

Interviewer: So then you're saying that men *do* have an easier time of it.

Belinda: Yeah. It *is* easier for men. But I have mixed feelings. Sometimes I think that I'm just making excuses for myself. What I ask myself is, am I good enough? Am I *as* good as the men? Perhaps I'm not. But I really believe that if I do the work necessary in the business world, I'll be able to be as successful as any man. I think that there's much more of a level playing field than there was before. There's much more opportunity now for women than when I was younger.

Interviewer: And, do you think successful women help other women?

Belinda: Yes, I do. Women tend to think of helping themselves and helping other people, too. And I hope that I can help to increase the opportunities for many young girls – as well as boys.

Interviewer: You want to help boys also?

Belinda: Of course! It's cool for everyone to be successful. And I do see progress in the future. I really do.

Narrator: Now complete the steps in your book.

Narrator: **Chapter 4, Gender Issues Today**
Page 55
Answering true/false questions, Step 2

Interviewer: I'd like to ask your opinion about how gender roles are changing. Do you think there's real equality now?

Farnsworth: That's absolutely not true. The first thing is that there is still a pay disparity. Women make only about seventy percent of the dollar that men earn. There have been changes in the last twenty years or so, but they've been relatively modest. And there's still that glass ceiling, where women hit this invisible barrier as they try to move up.

Interviewer: Could you give me an example of the glass ceiling?

Farnsworth: Well, look at this. I'm a social worker. Ninety percent of my colleagues are women. But both the CEO and his boss are men. So the top executives are men and, uh, the, you know, the lower paid levels, most of them are women. I think that men are much more likely to be raised with a sense of entitlement than women.

Interviewer: And what about equality at home?

Farnsworth: I don't think there's equality there, either. You see, I think that gender differences often operate on unconscious levels. It almost never occurs to men that they can do housework just as well as women, or take care of children – even if they're divorced and have custody of a child. But women have been parenting children alone forever. And women just *assume* that they can do it.

Interviewer: How has this affected you in your own life?

Farnsworth: Well, with both my children, from two different marriages, I was always the person who got up at night and gave the baby a bottle. I was always very actively involved with caring for my children, cooking for them. And I joined a playgroup with my son – twenty-five years ago! Incidentally, I was the only male involved, and I loved it.

Interviewer: Good for you!

Farnsworth: That was very, very different from my father's generation. My father had almost nothing to do with us, until we were eight or ten. He held us and gave us some smiles and so on, but he wasn't really an active parent. But I was determined to be a part of the joy of it all.

Interviewer: So what you're saying is that the situation has changed, but there's still inequality.

Farnsworth: Oh, yes. I think that's true. Absolutely!

Narrator: Now complete the steps in your book.

Narrator: **Chapter 4, Gender Issues Today**
Page 60
Note taking: Using telegraphic language, Step 2

Narrator: One.

Wendy Gavis: . . . it's a question of equality. For example, when people say "mankind," it sounds as if they're only talking about men, but when you say "human beings," or "people," then you include both men and women.

Narrator: Two.

Wendy Gavis: I, for one, would say that if we speak about people in certain ways, that definitely has an influence on the way we think about them. Imagine a little girl who grows up hearing "chairman, chairman, chairman." What is she going to think of when she hears this word? A man, of course.

Narrator: Three.

Wendy Gavis: The title of this lecture is *Gender and Language*. What I'm going to discuss, more specifically, is the topic of sexism in language, and how to avoid it.

Narrator: Four.

Wendy Gavis: Let's turn to the question of gender-specific terms. Many terms, like "mailman" or "policeman" are gender-specific. They all refer to men – yet there are women who do these jobs.

Narrator: Now complete the steps in your book.

Wendy Gavis: Good morning. Please take notes on today's lecture. Everyone should pick up his pen – or rather, everyone should pick up her pen. Or everyone should pick up his or her pen. Or her or his pen. Wait – let me start again. Everyone should pick up their pen – mm, is that correct?

You get my point, right? The title of this lecture is *Gender and Language.* What I'm going to discuss, more specifically, is the topic of sexism in language, and how to avoid it.

First, then, is it true that language can be sexist? The answer is yes, it can. Take the example of this word: Mr. What word has the same meaning for women? There is none. There's Mrs., which means "I'm married;" there's Miss, which means "I'm not married;" and then, since the 1970s, we've had Ms., which means "it's none of your business whether I'm married or not!" Well, not exactly, but you get my point.

Let's turn to the question of gender-specific terms. Many terms, like "mailman," or "policeman," are gender-specific. They all refer to men – yet there are women who do these jobs. So what do we do? Well, a safe option is to use what we call "gender-neutral" terms, such as "mail carrier" or "police officer."

Why should we use gender-neutral language? Well, first of all, because it describes the world the way it really is. If children grow up hearing the word "chairman," then they internalize the idea that all leaders are men – which isn't true. Secondly, it's a question of equality. For example, when people say "mankind," it sounds as if they're only talking about men, but when you say "human beings," or "people," then you include both men and women.

But vocabulary isn't the only problem. Grammar is a problem, too. Do you remember the example I gave at the beginning? "Everyone should pick up . . . blank . . . pen"? Well, I wasn't really making a joke. The fact is I have to choose a pronoun. And I don't want to give the impression that everyone in the room is male or female either. So I'm facing a dilemma.

What's the solution? Well, personally, I prefer to say: "Everyone should pick up their pen." I realize this is not grammatically correct, but it does avoid sexism. And you'll find that most university professors and writers would probably make the same choice that I do. Look at the newspaper, or look around you on the bus or on the subway. You'll see plural pronouns in places you might not expect.

Narrator: Now complete the steps in your book.

Wendy Gavis: Now I'd like to organize the second part of the lecture around your questions. I can see that some of you have questions on your mind, so please go ahead and ask them.

Student: Professor Gavis, I'm sorry, but is all this concern about language really important? I mean, aren't there more serious issues facing women today?

Wendy Gavis: You know, I understand what you're saying. And of course, there are many serious issues facing women. I mean, there are so many that I could mention: the AIDS crisis, workplace inequality, the way the mass media treats women – that is, the way they *stereotype* women, and so on. But I'd like to point out that in addition to these issues, the language question is also on the minds of international organizations such as the United Nations, who try *very* hard to avoid sexism in their publications. You see, the issue isn't just the words themselves, but the ideas *behind* the words.

Have you ever thought about the roles that boys and girls play in children's literature? It often seems that the boys are the ones having all the fun, having adventures, and so on, while the girls just stand in the background, smiling sweetly. You see, women tend to be pushed to the background in society. By focusing on the language we use about women, we may be able to change their expectations.

Student: I have a question about the relationship between the way we think and the way we talk. For example, if we say "chair" instead of "chairman," do you really think we'll start imagining more women in powerful positions?

Wendy Gavis: Again, that's a very interesting question. And yes, it's true that we don't completely understand the relationship between language and thought. So does what we say affect what we think? The answer is probably yes. I, for one, would say that if we speak about people in certain ways, that definitely has an influence on the way we think about them. Imagine a little girl who grows up hearing "chairman, chairman, chairman." What is she going to think of when she hears this word? A man, of course. But we must give young people the idea that women can also enter the professional world and be successful.

Any more questions?

Student: Professor Gavis, does this controversy about how we use language exist in other languages, too?

Wendy Gavis: Yes, it's definitely receiving more and more attention worldwide. But remember that the feminist movement, which is so active in the United States, has been a major force behind the move to avoid sexist language. It's a complicated issue, however, because the issues of gender in language change from one language to the next. For example, nouns don't have a gender in English, but there are two genders for nouns in Spanish – masculine and feminine. And German has three gender groups – some nouns are masculine, others are feminine, and there's a third category, which isn't masculine or feminine. So each language has its own gender issues.

You might want to take a look at some newspapers and magazines to see how they avoid sexism in English.

Well, we'll have to leave it there for today. Thank you.

Narrator: Now complete the steps in your book.

5

Narrator: Chapter 5, Mass Media Today
Page 67
Listening for specific information, Step 1

Narrator: One.

Man: Some very alarming new statistics show that the number of teens who drink is on the increase.

Narrator: Two.

Woman: Elsie Smith was interviewed by reporters yesterday because it was her birthday. She was one hundred and five years old!

Narrator: Three.

Man: New research indicates that mammal cloning is becoming easier. Opposition to cloning continues, however.

Narrator: Four.

Woman: The world title in distance running is dominated by runners from a small handful of countries. This year, runners from Kenya and Ethiopia will compete for the title.

Narrator: Five.

Man: Hundreds of people were injured as a major tornado ripped through the Midwest yesterday.

Narrator: Six.

Woman: A small town in upstate New York is welcoming immigrants from South America. The mayor says that they will be a big help in improving the economy.

Narrator: Seven.

Man: If you smoke, you may soon be paying more for your habit. The tax on cigarettes is due to rise again next month.

Narrator: Eight.

Woman: There may be new hope for people suffering from certain types of skin cancer. A new drug that scientists have been developing has been approved for testing.

Narrator: Now complete the steps in your book.

**Narrator: Chapter 5, Mass Media Today
Page 69
Answering multiple-choice questions,
Step 2**

Interviewer: Hi, Carol. I'd like to get your opinion about news in the United States.

Carol: Well, I have very strong opinions about it. We *think* we're getting the news, but it's really just entertainment. It's based on what's going to keep people tuned in, like plastic surgery or celebrities. They actually tease you to get you to watch the news with those stories, because I think they think Americans get bored with international news.

Interviewer: You're talking about news on TV.

Carol: Uh, yeah. They say: "Tune in at 11, find out how this woman lost weight." And that kind of keeps people watching – and that's what they call "news." But what about major political problems? Those don't get reported in the way they should be – they don't get reported enough.

Interviewer: Yeah, I-I see what you're saying . . .

Carol: The other thing that bothers me about the news is that it's shallow. Like, there are these people doing voice-overs. But the voice-overs have the same tone as people who do it for movies. It's like "Six Guns to Kill" and then it's like "Plastic Surgery at 11." And it's the same voice, the same style for those two stories. It's equating those types of information. It's all like entertainment.

Interviewer: Do you think entertainment is more interesting than news?

Carol: Good question. I actually think we've gotten used to the idea that news should be just as entertaining as the movies. Like a sitcom. And it should be quick, and sort of like instant gratification.

Interviewer: What do you mean by instant gratification?

Carol: It's something that doesn't require you to think. Easy information. Something that makes you feel like you're learning something, but you really aren't. So, it's quick and it's shallow. And the TV news has to be reported by news anchors who are physically attractive. If they're not attractive, viewers complain.

Interviewer: Well, do you think newspapers give you better news coverage than TV?

Carol: I think newspapers are better, because they're more in depth. But then who has time to really read them? And what's difficult about news in general is . . . see, I'm criticizing what's being reported, but the main problem is what's *not* being reported. And that's hard to criticize, because you don't know what's not there. And I think papers are guilty of that.

Interviewer: Do you get any news from radio or the Internet? Are they better? I mean, are there *any* good places to get news?

Carol: I do think there are better places. But you have to spend time finding them. And people need quick access. If you want to get specialized news, you have to go to special radio stations or websites, and I don't even know what those are.

Interviewer: So, where do you get your news?

Carol: Mostly on TV. That's the thing. I realize I'm being sucked into it. So I'm critical of it, but it's OK because I *know* I'm being sucked in!

Narrator: Now complete the steps in your book.

Interviewer: Hi, Shari. I'd like to get your opinion about the news.

Shari: OK. Well, I get most of my news on the Internet, but I read papers, too.

Interviewer: And what do you think about the news in the newspaper?

Shari: What I notice about the papers is that the news is really depressing, especially the main stories – you have bombings, and accidents, and people killing people. I find more and more that the news in the United States is getting focused on negative things. It's always a disaster of some sort.

Interviewer: So you think it's very negative.

Shari: Yeah, and there's something else. I like to read about international news, but it seems that people here aren't really that interested in it. I read somewhere, I can't remember – that it's a prestige thing, to cover the international news.

Interviewer: And you don't think people in the United States like international news?

Shari: No. I don't. But because I've lived in so many countries around the world, I *am* interested in international news. The news in Korea is from everywhere – the United States, Europe, Japan, China. Anyway, what I *like* about newspapers are the arts and culture sections. And the human interest stories, which can be really uplifting. I like to read about people. For example, there was a story about some crime in the park, but now they're examining that case again, and it turns out that the five young people who they thought did it might be innocent, actually. It was shocking that the judicial system had failed in the beginning, but I'm glad they finally found out that those young people were innocent.

Interviewer: So you liked that story.

Shari: Yeah, I mean, that kind of news, people could actually read it and feel positive, like you could really improve the system, or whatever – compared to news that's depressing and you feel helpless – you can't do anything about it.

Interviewer: Frank, what do you think about the news?

Frank: Well, I don't know about the *news,* but I like the *newspaper.* I get one every day. I walk over to the store and I buy the paper, I go home, I sit down in my chair and I really enjoy reading it.

Interviewer: What do you read?

Frank: Well, first I look at the front page. And then, I turn to the sports section to find out how my teams are doing! I read all the articles about them. Usually I've seen those games anyway so I like to compare what the writer says with what I think. And then I read the main stories, especially the scandals! But what I *really* enjoy are the crossword puzzles. I'll sit for hours trying to figure some of them out. I have this electronic dictionary I sometimes use for the clues.

Interviewer: And what do you do if you can't get a word?

Frank: Well, then I'll take a break. I usually get everything eventually. You learn to see how these people think. It's the same with journalists. You get to know what their opinions and reactions are going to be.

Interviewer: You mean in the regular news?

Frank: Yeah. You see, I do read the articles about what the government's doing, and what's happening, but what you have to realize is that reporters are just people, like you. They have their own opinions about what's going on. So you have to take what they say with a grain of salt. It's a lot of half-truths they write to make you think what *they* want you to think about. You can get the basic information, but you have to use your own ideas to analyze the news. A lot of the time it's really biased.

Narrator: Now complete the steps in your book.

Narrator: One.

Sarah Coleman: Nowadays, more than ever before, we are surrounded by news.

Narrator: Two.

Sarah Coleman: In fact, so many new stories appear every day that it's impossible to keep up with them!

Narrator: Three.

Sarah Coleman: First of all, there are different kinds of journalists.

Narrator: Four.

Sarah Coleman: Sometimes, journalists are called reporters because they "report" the news.

Narrator: Five.

Sarah Coleman: Usually, unplanned events are more exciting!

Narrator: Six.

Sarah Coleman: However, it's important not to report too much personal information or anything that is scandalous.

Narrator: Now complete the steps in your book.

Narrator: **Chapter 5, Mass Media Today**
Page 77
Note taking: Choosing a format for organizing your notes, Step 2

Sarah Coleman: Nowadays – more than ever before – we are surrounded by news. You can get the news on radio, on television, in newspapers, and on the Internet. In fact, so many new stories appear every day that it's impossible to keep up with them! And behind all of these stories, there's a journalist. First of all, there are different kinds of journalists, like entertainment journalists, sports journalists, and crime journalists, and they all work hard to deliver the news, twenty-four hours a day.

So how exactly do they find and write stories?

Let's look at the work of one type of journalist: a city reporter. (Sometimes, journalists are called reporters because they "report" the news.) So a city reporter is a person assigned to find and write stories about local news. How does the reporter do her work? Well, to begin with, she should keep in contact with lots of different organizations: the local police and fire departments, the offices of local politicians, and religious and civic organizations in the neighborhood.

Once the reporter has a good relationship with these organizations, she can call them to see what's happening, or they might call her to tell her about something that's going on. There are two kinds of stories she could write about. The first is a planned event for which the reporter can anticipate many of the details. For example, a politician could be opening a new department store. The second is an unplanned event, for example, a fire or a crime. Usually, unplanned events are more exciting!

Let's look at one kind of unplanned event: a crime. Imagine that a fight breaks out between four men in a neighborhood bar and one of the men threatens another with a knife. The reporter will probably see a few lines about the crime in the police log. Once she knows where it happened, she can go to the scene of the crime and interview people. The first person she will want to interview is a police officer, so that she can get the facts. There are four very important facts that every reader wants to know at the beginning of every story: (1) What happened? (2) When did it happen? (3) Where did it happen? and, (4) Who was involved?

Once the reporter has the basic facts of the story, she can begin to interview witnesses. When you're interviewing witnesses, it's very important to get each witness's full name and some other details –

perhaps the person's job or age. These details will make the story more interesting and credible. However, it's important not to report too much personal information or anything that is scandalous.

When the reporter has finished interviewing people, she'll go back to the newsroom to write the story. At that point, she might talk to her editor to decide whether she has a good story. Together, the reporter and editor must decide whether the reporter has enough facts and material to make a good story. Is it clear what happened and why?

Narrator: Now complete the steps in your book.

Narrator: Chapter 5, Mass Media Today
Page 80
Note taking: Choosing a format for organizing your notes, Step 1

Sarah Coleman: The single most important question of all is whether or not the story is accurate. If a newspaper publishes a story that isn't supported by facts, and somebody finds a mistake, then the newspaper's reputation will be damaged for a long time. For example, if the paper publishes a story saying that Bill Jones started the fight, and later it turns out that Fred Porter started the fight, there would be a problem. First of all, the public would have been misinformed, and people might decide not to buy that paper in the future. Secondly, Bill Jones could decide to sue the paper for misrepresenting his character. That's called libel, and it's something judges take very seriously.

That's why many newspapers insist on having every controversial fact in a story supported by two different sources. If two people who don't know each other both tell the reporter that Bill Jones started the fight, then the newspaper feels it can publish the story.

But checking every fact with two different sources takes a long time, and there isn't much time in the news world.

Yesterday's news isn't worth much to the public, and every newspaper wants to be the first to publish a story. A reporter who has a big story will always want to publish it as soon as possible, so it's the editor's job to check that the reporter has done her work thoroughly and that there are no uncorroborated facts.

But let's suppose the reporter has done her job well. She's checked all the facts and she knows she's got interesting interviews. Now she just has to write the story! Easy, right? Well, not always, remember how quickly most people read newspapers. A journalist must know how to organize a difficult story and present it very clearly, in language that's simple but very effective.

When the story is written, it goes into the computer. Somebody checks that the story is grammatically accurate, and somebody else checks it for typing mistakes. Then a photograph is chosen to go with the story, and the editor-in-chief decides what page of the newspaper to put the story on.

And what makes a good story? Well, there are three main things. First of all, the story has to be new. If it happened three months ago, it isn't news. Second, it has to be unusual. There's an old saying in the newsroom: If a dog bites a man, it isn't news. But if a man bites a dog, that's news! Third, it has to be something interesting that your readers want to know about. After all, if they don't want to know about it, they won't buy your newspaper.

Narrator: Now complete the steps in your book.

Narrator: Chapter 6, The Influence of the Media
Page 85
Listening for specific information, Step 2

Narrator: Chapter 6, The Influence of the Media
Page 83
Recording numerical information, Step 2

Man: The first area includes the United States, Canada, Europe, Australia, and Japan. In these countries, there are forty or more TVs per one hundred people.

Area 2 includes Brazil, Russia, South Korea, and the People's Republic of China. In this area, there are between twenty and forty TVs per one hundred people.

The next area includes Mexico, Central America, and part of South America. Part of Africa and most of the Middle East are also in Area 3. This area, which includes many countries in the developing world, has between eight and twenty TVs per one hundred people.

Finally, we come to Area 4 – most of Africa and all of India. Here, there are fewer than eight TVs per one hundred people.

Narrator: Now complete the steps in your book.

Narrator: Chapter 6, The Influence of the Media
Page 85
Listening for specific information, Step 1

Narrator: One. Eddie.

Interviewer: Hi Eddie. Tell me how often you play video games.

Eddie: I don't know, maybe a couple of hours a week. In the summer time it's more, maybe five, six hours a week.

Narrator: Two. Leslie.

Leslie: Well, I guess I've mixed feelings about cell phones. They used to bother me a lot, but now I have one.

Narrator: Three. Ralph.

Ralph: I really like watching action movies. Kung Fu movies, adventure, stuff like that.

Narrator: Now complete the steps in your book.

Interviewer: Hi, Eddie. Tell me how often you play video games.

Eddie: I don't know, maybe a couple of hours a week. In the summer time it's more, maybe five, six hours a week.

Interviewer: Don't you think there's a lot of violence in video games?

Eddie: Yeah, well, I try not to play those games. I only like sports games. I hate those gun ones where you just walk around and kill people.

Interviewer: Why? Do you think they have a bad effect on you?

Eddie: I don't think a bad effect, maybe a wasteful effect. I feel like when I play, I'm wasting the day away. I think video games restrict the things kids do, like read. Kids can become addicted to them. They just sit and do video games all day.

Interviewer: So you think they do have a bad effect.

Eddie: I don't know – a bad effect? Not for teenagers, I don't think. Maybe they could be dangerous for little kids, because they haven't been alive for that long, and their minds aren't fully developed.

Interviewer: And what about big kids? Do big kids know the difference between fantasy and reality?

Eddie: Yeah, definitely.

Interviewer: But what about all the violence?

Eddie: Well, most kids like the feeling of killing things in video games. But it's part of the game. It's not real. Video games can be very entertaining, but it's not good if you overuse them. The reason isn't because they'll make you deranged, just that they make you waste time. I don't play any violent games, myself. But I know a lot of people who do – and they don't really have a negative effect. They just make the kid a little bit more antisocial. They don't make people want to kill each other.

Interviewer: Leslie, can you tell me if there's any form of media that has a particular influence on you?

Leslie: Well, I guess I've mixed feelings about cell phones. They used to bother me a lot, but now I have one.

Interviewer: Why didn't you like them?

Leslie: I used to think they were just trendy, a status symbol thing, and too expensive. But I think there are other dangers with cell phones.

Interviewer: Like what?

Leslie: Like driving while talking on the cell phone. When I was coming home from college for Thanksgiving break, the bus driver was talking on his cell phone the whole way, and it, it really upset me. Here he was . . . the weather was really bad, and he was just talking on the phone, and I was really scared, like I didn't think I was gonna get home!

Interviewer: Wow. That does sound dangerous!

Leslie: Yeah, but I think there are benefits too. I finally bought one because I need people to get in touch with me about school, or about work. And for my mom. She works a lot, she's away from home a lot, so it's great for her to have a cell phone to call us at home, to keep tabs on us. And, you know, we can call her, too.

Interviewer: Ralph, you watch a lot of movies, right?

Ralph: Yeah. I really like watching action movies. Kung Fu movies, adventure, stuff like that. They're interesting.

Interviewer: Do you watch them with your family?

Ralph: Yeah, but you've got to keep an eye on the movies. If they're too bad, I won't let my girls watch. I say, hey, let's go to the park or something.

Interviewer: Why? Are you worried about them getting bad messages?

Ralph: Oh, yeah. You gotta check out the program. See, the movies they have on now are not the same as they used to have years ago, you know? They've gotten a lot more violent. And all of those special graphics make them look more real, too. And then there's the sex. A lot of movies are full of sex. So the parents, they need to check out the movies that the kids are watching. Except the movies with the heroes, now they're all right, where they catch the bad guy. Those movies are good for 'em.

Interviewer: Do you think kids copy the actions of the heroes?

Ralph: Ah, not really. But at least those movies don't have much sex. See, the young kids can't really understand that TV is only imaginary. They think it's real.

Narrator: Now complete the steps in your book.

Narrator: **Chapter 6, The Influence of the Media**
Page 87
Listening for specific information, Step 1

Narrator: One. Vanessa.

Vanessa: Um, let's see. Well, personally, I'm *really* shocked to watch the regular TV news, because it's paid for by these big corporations. And it's completely drained of all real information.

Narrator: Two. Felix.

Interviewer: Felix, how much TV do *you* watch a day?

Felix: Oh, I can't say, but the older you get, the more you get into it. It's very entertaining.

Narrator: Three. Richard.

Richard: Well, I do have a confession to make. The only modern form of media I really like is the jet plane. I mean, I know it's not "the media," but I really consider it to be a form of communication.

Narrator: Now complete the steps in your book.

Narrator: Chapter 6, The Influence of the Media
Page 87
Listening for specific information, Step 2

Interviewer: Vanessa, what kind of influence do you think the media has on us?

Vanessa: Um, let's see. Well, personally, I'm *really* shocked to watch the regular TV news, because it's paid for by these big corporations. And it's completely drained of all real information. The TV news is totally biased and only shows certain things. You can't get a clear picture of what's really going on.

Interviewer: And who's responsible for that?

Vanessa: The corporate and political interests. The news is totally manipulated. They're not going to tell us anything that isn't prepackaged. It's infotainment, isn't that what they call it now?

Interviewer: Infotainment?

Vanessa: Yeah. It's a combination of the words information and entertainment. I mean, during a war now, you see these huge maps and the planes that go zooming around. They treat war like a video game.

Interviewer: And Felix, how much TV do *you* watch a day?

Felix: Oh, I can't say, but the older you get, the more you get into it. It's very entertaining. I usually watch good movies. Sometimes a sitcom, but a lotta sports. I'm really into sports, particularly women's sports. I think this is the time of women in sports. Sports give you a lotta character.

Interviewer: Do you think television has a positive effect on people?

Felix: Well, it depends. There are a lot of educational programs that help kids. You know, nature programs.

Interviewer: Anything else?

Felix: I also like a good "whodunit." I like cartoons, too. You have to look for what is positive. But parents are the nucleus of the family, so they have to pay attention to what their kids are watching. Especially when the kids are in their formative years.

Interviewer: Richard, I know you have strong feelings about the media.

Richard: I do. I've never had a television in my life. I grew up before television was really common and I just don't have time for it. I think you have to look at the trade-off for whatever you do.

Interviewer: What do you mean by *trade-off*?

Richard: What it costs, not only in money, but in terms of what it does to your life. I have no real machines in my apartment. Well, I-I *do* have an FM radio,

Interviewer: Yeah, what do you listen to?

Richard: Oh, weather reports, ah, good music. And I have a telephone *now*, but I lived for eight years without one.

Interviewer: Eight years without a telephone?

Richard: Well, I discovered there were telephones on every street corner and I really didn't need one for anything.

Interviewer: Do you have a computer?

Richard: I do not own a computer. Because when I go on the Internet, I'm always disappointed. You see, I think modern technology destroys all the beauty and meaning in life. The machine gets in the way. And I don't want to be part of a machine. That's not the way I want to live my life.

Interviewer: Aren't there any good things that the modern media bring us? I don't know . . . closer contact with other people?

Richard: Well, I do have a confession to make. The only modern form of media I really like is the jet plane. I mean, I know it's not "the media," but I really consider it to be a form of communication. It has allowed me to travel all over the world. I get great enjoyment out of traveling. I link up with people from foreign countries, I meet them, I talk to them, and so in that way, the jet plane has improved international communication, much more than fax or e-mail will ever do.

Interviewer: What an interesting idea! Thank you, Richard.

Narrator: Now complete the steps in your book.

Narrator: **Chapter 6, The Influence of the Media**
Page 92
Note taking: Organizing your notes as a map, Step 2

Dedra Smith: Fifteen years ago, if you heard the words "mass media," you probably immediately thought of television, newspapers, magazines, and the radio.

But today, if you made a list of the mass media you use, you would have to add newer technologies such as cable, satellite TV, PDAs or personal digital assistants, and the Internet.

And of course, technology has brought us some wonderful things, and I personally wouldn't want to live without it. But all these new advances bring us dangers that we should be aware of.

There's a lot of violence in TV shows, and many people worry about its effect on us.

In addition to making us violent, TV can also make us passive.

Third, using the media can become very addictive.

Narrator: Now complete the steps in your book.

Narrator: **Chapter 6, The Influence of the Media**
Page 93
Note taking: Organizing your notes as a map, Step 2

Dedra Smith: Fifteen years ago, if you heard the words "mass media," you probably immediately thought of television, newspapers, magazines, and the radio. But today, if you made a list of the mass media you use, you would have to add newer technologies such as cable, satellite TV, PDAs or personal digital assistants, and the Internet. In today's world, we are surrounded by technology that allows us to communicate with others. And of course, technology has brought us some wonderful things, and I personally wouldn't want to

live without it. But all these new advances bring us dangers that we should be aware of. Let's begin by discussing three of these dangers: violence, passivity, and addiction.

There's a lot of violence in TV shows, and many people worry about its effect on us. For example, almost every home in the United States has a color television, and according to a recent study, TV is on in the average household for seven hours and thirty-seven minutes every day. And many people are afraid that children and adolescents are especially susceptible to this violence. In 1993, for example, a young boy jumped out of a window after seeing a superhero do the same thing on TV while he was chasing an enemy. And what about the movie where kids set a subway booth on fire? Some teenagers saw that movie and then they did the same thing. Tragically, the man working at the booth died as a result of the fire.

In addition to making us violent, TV can also make us passive. You've probably heard the term "couch potato." It refers to a person who daydreams for hours in front of the TV. When we are in this passive state, we may not be able to distinguish between fantasy and reality and we may make bad decisions about important things in our lives.

Third, using the media can become very addictive. For example, how many Internet users can say that they quickly go online, find what they need, and get off again? That's just not the case for most of us, who wander through cyberspace, clicking here and there and wasting a lot of time in the process. If you check your e-mail more than three or four times a day, you might want to ask yourself if you really need all that communication. And cell phones – which these days can also be used to go online – are highly addictive, as well.

Narrator: Now complete the steps in your book.

Narrator: **Chapter 6, The Influence of the Media**
Page 95
Note taking: Organizing your notes as a map, Step 2

Dedra Smith: The fourth danger we should be concerned about is the increase in advertising. You see, the media is not only interested in providing information or entertainment, but also selling space or time to advertisers. You used to be able to enjoy a TV show, or relax and read a magazine, and there wasn't too much advertising. Now, however, it seems that advertising is the main goal. The content of a TV program or a magazine is just an excuse, or a kind of wrapping, for the advertising. There's an essential marketing relationship between the media, the advertiser, and the user, and it exists whatever the media. Even print media, which is one of the least technological forms of communication, has a high percentage of ads.

On TV, of course, we're used to being bombarded by endless commercials every eight minutes. Many of us use our remote control to zap out the advertising with the "mute" button, or simply channel surf to find someplace we can escape from the ads. But the advertisers have found many ways to get their message across to you, anyway. They use what is called "product placement," which means that they put products right in the middle of a show. For example, the hero of the show might be drinking a particular soft drink, like Coca-Cola or Dr. Pepper. Or he might be wearing a pair of shoes with the name Nike or Adidas. You can't escape from this form of advertising unless you just turn off your set.

The problem is not just that we are being bombarded by advertising, but that the media is invading our privacy. Advertisers are more and more interested in getting private information about individuals. Every time you use your credit card, you're giving away information about yourself. Advertisers have the ability to gather statistical data about people like you: potential consumers.

Think about this for a moment: Have you ever gotten junk mail from a company you never heard of? Where did they get your address? Have you ever gotten a phone call during dinner from some company trying to sell you something? Where did they get your telephone number? Well, information about you can be compiled and sold to other companies. And advertisers can study what you buy, where you buy it, and how much of it you buy, and figure out the best way to make you buy more! On the Internet, many websites are working extra hard to collect information about you. You can be tracked if you make a few visits to any website, and the data can be used to learn more about your habits, interests, and other behavior.

We are surrounded everywhere by a message that tells us that we can be better, more successful, more popular, and altogether happier if we just have more. I believe we need to step back once in a while and ask ourselves if this message is true. *Is* it true? *Are* we what we buy? What if we couldn't buy anything, ever? Who would we be?

Narrator: Now complete the steps in your book.

7

Narrator: **Chapter 7, Crime and Criminals**
Page 100
Building background knowledge on the topic: technical terms, Step 1

Narrator: One.

Woman: A gold watch and a necklace were stolen from a home on Woodfield Avenue. The criminals entered the house through a bathroom window.

Narrator: Two.

Man: A man was arrested at midnight on Harper Street because he was carrying a handgun without a license. He was taken to the police station for questioning.

Narrator: Three.

Woman: There's breaking news in the sexual assault case that we reported last week. Police have charged a man in connection with two similar cases that took place in the same neighborhood.

Narrator: Four.

Man: A woman in her late thirties was found taking items from the local pharmacy. She was caught on camera as she was putting the items in her pocket.

Narrator: Five.

Woman: Two teenage boys were arrested for setting their school on fire! They entered the school after classes were over, and set fire to the teacher's lounge. Luckily, no one was hurt.

Narrator: Six.

Man: A car that was stolen from a supermarket parking lot was found near an old house by the railroad tracks. No one has been arrested yet in connection with the crime.

Narrator: Seven.

Woman: A jealous ex-boyfriend has been charged in the killing of two young people in their twenties. The couple had been planning to get married.

Narrator: Now complete the steps in your book.

**Narrator: Chapter 7, Crime and Criminals Page 102
Answering true/false questions, Step 2**

Interviewer: I'd like to ask both of you – now that you have a young child – whether you worry about the level of crime in the city.

Evelina: Luckily, I've never actually been struck by crime. But now that we have Daniel, I've become more conscious of it.

Interviewer: What do you mean?

Evelina: Well, personally, it doesn't affect me that much, but I hear so many stories and I see it on the TV news, so I'm aware of it and concerned about it. Sometimes I'm out late at night, and I see big groups of kids roaming the streets. And that frightens me.

Interviewer: And you, Arpad?

Arpad: Yeah, I mean, it depends. If it's a rowdy teenage group, I go over to the other side of the street. I'm tall, but still I try to avoid them.

Evelina: And what I think is that they should be doing something else.

Interviewer: Do you worry that violence could affect your life?

Evelina: I do, to be honest. Every time I get on the subway, I'm afraid that someone in the car could have a gun. Guns might not be visible, but they're everywhere, and at any minute, people can lose control. Guns are my biggest fear. I think guns are the biggest problem in the city.

Interviewer: And you, Arpad?

Arpad: Well, I've never seen anyone with a gun – and much less seen a shooting – but just last week someone got shot in a bookstore! In the safest part of the city! It's very random: that's what worries me. There was another incident where a kid was asleep, and there was a shot from the apartment next door that went through the wall, and the bullet struck him in the leg. You're not even safe in your own house.

Interviewer: Why do you think there *is* so much crime?

Arpad: Because kids think guns are ordinary. They're available. They're just facts of life. It's a recipe for disaster.

Evelina: I think that kids don't have enough contact with their parents. Basically kids who get into gangs don't have that much contact with other people . . . you know what I'm trying to say?

Arpad: I agree with Evelina. Parents are the main people that need to be responsible for their children. My sister's a teacher, and she says it's amazing . . . some parents think that school is responsible for teaching kids values. But that's not what I think.

Evelina: So many problems come from the fact that parents can't spend enough time with their kids.

Arpad: And gun control should be the government's responsibility. If there were fewer guns, that would definitely bring crime down.

Evelina: Yeah, the government has such a slack attitude toward guns. I really agree with Arpad.

Narrator: Now complete the steps in your book.

Narrator: Chapter 7, Crime and Criminals
Page 103
Retelling what you have heard, Step 2

Interviewer: Gail, I know you've been the victim of a crime.

Gail: Unfortunately, yes. Once I was mugged by some young kids.

Interviewer: What happened?

Gail: I was going home late at night and I couldn't see a single person on the street. And it was winter, oh, it was *so cold*! So I had my scarf wrapped around my face. And then – suddenly – I walked straight into these three guys – they looked about fourteen or fifteen. And they said something threatening like "Give us all your money, we're gonna kill you!" and I'm looking at them because they look so young. And I'm thinking what on earth are you doing? They said "Blah, blah, blah, blah" and I said, "Listen, it's very cold, give me a second, I have to take off my gloves."

Interviewer: You must have been really scared!

Gail: Well, I open my purse, and all I've got is a few dollars. I was so nervous. And I say, "Here it is." And they say, "Four dollars?" Yeah, it's four dollars. And they say, "That's all you have?"

Interviewer: So, so, then what happened?

Gail: Well, I gave them the money, and I just went home. But I felt so bad. You know, I really had mixed feelings about it. I wanted to say, guys, what are you doing? You

know, go home! You're ruining your lives! And I think, why are those kids on the street, doing things they're not supposed to? Something stupid, really stupid – that could lead to something worse.

Interviewer: Why do you think kids get involved in stealing?

Gail: I don't know. I mean, it was only four dollars! You look at kids getting involved in this kind of small crime, and you think, who's responsible? I don't know what they were doing out on the street at that time of night.

Interviewer: Did you report the crime?

Gail: No, I didn't. Kids like that don't need prosecuting, they need parenting. They need someone to put them on the right path. These kids really need, you know, *help*.

Interviewer: In what way?

Gail: Well, kids are so vulnerable. They have to get a lot of supervision. There are these kids hanging out on the street, doing things they're not supposed to. It's almost a macho type of thing. But I think if these kids had more self-esteem they wouldn't behave in that way. We have to find ways to help these kinds of kids have good futures. Then they wouldn't commit crimes.

Interviewer: What about you, Tom? What was your experience?

Tom: Well, actually, I was robbed several times. The worst time was when my apartment was burglarized. I got home and saw the lock on my door had been broken and the apartment was ransacked.

Interviewer: What was taken?

Tom: They took my camera, my stereo, my paperwork. I lost irreplaceable personal items.

Interviewer: Were you scared?

Tom: No, I was angry. And I felt helpless, because I knew I could never find out what really happened. And I knew I'd never get my stuff back. It's like a feeling of violation when you know that someone has broken into your private space and taken your things. I called the police so that I could have a record of what was stolen for tax purposes. But, ah, they never caught the thief.

Interviewer: And that wasn't the first time you were robbed.

Tom: No. I've had things taken by pickpockets. Once someone took my wallet on the subway and there was a letter from my girlfriend in it that I liked to carry around with me. Not really important, I suppose, but it had symbolic value and when something like that happens, you lose a part of your past. That time, I felt angry at *myself* because they always tell you not to put your wallet in your back pocket.

Narrator: Now complete the steps in your book.

Narrator: Chapter 7, Crime and Criminals
Page 108
Note taking: Clarifying your notes, Step 2

Michael Anglin: Crime can be divided into two main categories: misdemeanors and felonies. A misdemeanor is broadly defined as a crime that is punishable with more than fifteen days in prison, but less than one year. A felony carries a term of imprisonment of more than one year. When a person who commits a misdemeanor or a felony is caught, that person – who is called a defendant or the accused – goes through a legal process that ends with a judge or a jury finding him either guilty or innocent. If the person is found guilty, then the judge decides what the punishment should be.

Narrator: Now complete the steps in your book.

Narrator: Chapter 7, Crime and Criminals
Page 109
Note taking: Clarifying your notes, Step 1

Michael Anglin: Crime can be divided into two main categories: misdemeanors and felonies. A misdemeanor is broadly defined as a crime that is punishable with more than fifteen days in prison, but less than one year. A felony carries a term of

imprisonment of more than one year. When a person who commits a misdemeanor or a felony is caught, that person – who is called a defendant or the accused – goes through a legal process that ends with a judge or a jury finding him either guilty or innocent. If the person is found guilty, then the judge decides what the punishment should be.

Let me begin by talking about types of felonies. Some of the more serious felonies include burglary, robbery, arson, kidnapping, rape, and murder. These crimes are so serious that anyone found guilty will spend some time in prison. A misdemeanor, on the other hand, could be pickpocketing, fare evasion, or something of that nature. But sometimes a crime that is a misdemeanor in one part of the country might be a felony in another part of the country.

Another way in which people may classify crime is by using the terms white-collar crime or blue-collar crime. White-collar crime refers to crime committed by salaried employees in businesses and corporations. It includes tax fraud and embezzlement and it can involve large sums of money and affect millions of people. One of the main types of white-collar crime is corporate crime. Corporate crime is committed by people of high social status who work in corporations. Corporate crime is very difficult to prosecute for two main reasons: First, because it's difficult to prove who's responsible; and second, because the criminals are usually wealthy and powerful. An example of corporate crime that *was* successfully prosecuted concerns the tobacco industry in the United States. The tobacco industry was found guilty of causing the deaths of thousands of people who smoked cigarettes. As punishment, tobacco companies have had to pay millions of dollars to the victims' families.

The crimes you're more likely to hear about are blue-collar crimes: such as burglary, car theft, pickpocketing, and so on. Perhaps we hear more about these crimes because they happen more often. However, white-collar crime can have a greater impact on our society.

Crime has always existed in society, but today there are new kinds of crimes. One example is the use of computers to steal identities. As more people have access to computers, the more likely it is for your identity to be stolen. If this happens, criminals may open several credit card accounts and bank accounts in your name. And, of course, they won't pay the bill, which means that your credit will be ruined, and that's *very* difficult to correct.

Narrator: Now complete the steps in your book.

Narrator: Chapter 7, Crime and Criminals
Page 111
Note taking: Using your notes to answer test questions, Step 2

Michael Anglin: As long as there has been crime, there have been ways to solve it. One of the oldest methods is interrogation, a method in which the police question people who might have committed the crime or who might have information about the crime. Interrogation can help the police to establish many basic facts. But modern techniques for solving crime include more complex scientific methods.

Let me talk first about a system often called "crime hotlines." In some cases, where law enforcement personnel have difficulty finding a criminal, they turn to private citizens for help in solving a crime. This system allows people to make a phone call or access a website and give information to the police anonymously. This can often be effective when people are afraid to give information in public. Sometimes a family member may have committed the crime and another family member finally decides to call the police and give the information they have.

Second, fingerprinting. Each person's fingerprint is unique. The ancient Chinese used fingerprints to sign legal papers. What better way to identify an individual? Yet it was only in the late nineteenth century that fingerprints were first used to identify criminals. A variety of scientific techniques make it possible for fingerprints to be "lifted" from most surfaces. Then they can be compared to fingerprints the police have on file.

A relatively new technique that crime fighters are now using is called psychological profiling. Criminal psychologists look at the crime and the way it was committed. Based on this information, they try to understand the personality and motivation of the person who committed the crime. Then they can focus their search on people who match this profile.

In some cases, private citizens are finding ways to solve crimes as well. With a little knowledge of electronics, anyone can put hidden cameras in a home or office. In the 1990s, as an example, there were some cases where nannies were accused of abusing the children they were paid to care for. Hidden cameras were used to prove the nannies' guilt. However, the technique is controversial because it involves issues of privacy.

Finally, let me discuss DNA. Of the most recent crime-solving techniques used, DNA is proving very effective. Each person, with the exception of identical siblings, has a unique DNA coding system. So, if criminals leave anything that can be tested at the scene of a crime – such as blood or hair – they can be identified. DNA was used to solve a crime for the first time in England in 1987. Since that time, it has become widely used and is considered ninety-nine percent accurate. DNA testing can also be used to prove that a person is innocent. Many prisoners have been released because the DNA evidence proves that they did not commit the crime of which they were convicted.

Narrator: Now complete the steps in your book.

Narrator: CD [Cassette] 3
   Chapter 8, Controlling Crime
   Page 114
   Listening for opinions, Step 2

Narrator: One.
Woman: That's really terrible! What a horrible crime!

Narrator: Two.
Man: Mmm. I don't know. I guess the woman was wrong. After all, she was taking the son against the father's wishes.

Narrator: Three.
Woman: Well that's a bad thing to do, at least nobody was hurt. But I think those kids should definitely be punished!

Narrator: Four.
Woman: Well, I don't know if that's so bad. Who knows – maybe they had a good reason for refusing to pay the rent.

Narrator: Five.
Man: That's awful! It's horrible how someone can trick an old person that way. Poor woman!

Narrator: Six.
Man: That's not all that bad. I know a lot of teenagers who have done things like that.

Narrator: Now complete the steps in your book.

Narrator: **Chapter 8, Controlling Crime**
   Page 117
   Listening for specific information, Step 2

Interviewer: Hi, David. I just saw a program on TV that said that juvenile crime was increasing. And I wanted to ask your opinion about how to stop, well, how to prevent juvenile crime because I know that you work with a lot of young people.
David: Well first, I think the media exacerbates the problem. And so does the school system. Where I live, we have thousands of security guards in the schools, and metal detectors too, and the kids get searched as they go into school. Now all of that presents the wrong message. The kids don't feel like they're going to school: they feel like they're going to jail, and so they're more likely to lash out and become violent. I think it's a cause and effect relationship. The students get violent because the system makes them like that.
Interviewer: So you're saying that the messages kids get from the media – and even from school – are responsible for making them do bad things.
David: Yes , I am. I think that every young person is essentially good. I mean, you see violent students – students who are violent in class – but put them on a one-to-one basis, and they're usually very friendly. It's not that they're really bad. It's that they're a product of their environment. If you give them a more caring environment, you really can change the kind of actions they take.
Interviewer: Well, what about all the social support systems?
David: You see, the problem is that social support systems have really fallen apart. Take, for example, Big Brother/Big Sister programs. Or after-school programs. You know, and I don't mean just letting them stay in school until 6 o'clock, doing whatever they want. They should be doing healthy, supervised activities. A structured program of activities. Instructional programs. Or it could be athletics. A lot of our schools used to have football teams, or basketball teams, or baseball teams, but the funding for programs like those has been cut. They've been eliminated. So that leaves a child with a lot of energy, and nothing to do with it.
Interviewer: What do the Big Brother/Big Sister programs do?
David: Well, they have people a little older, say in their twenties, who are willing to spend time on an individual basis with a student in middle school or in high school. See, the

problem is that a lot of kids don't get the one-on-one attention they need. But kids need to see that somebody really cares about them.

Interviewer: But what about kids who really *do* commit crimes? Stealing, pickpocketing, or drug abuse – or something worse. I mean, you do get cases where kids become involved in really serious crimes. I mean, what should be done with kids like that?

David: Well, let me say that preventing crime is definitely better than punishing it. It's better to have good role models and stop crime before it starts. But we also need harsher punishments. You see some countries where drug crimes carry a maximum sentence of twenty years or life imprisonment. And the crime numbers go down very fast! Having stronger punishment does reduce crime. But you have to be sure that the punishments are fair. We're talking about juvenile crime, but white-collar crime needs to be punished, too.

Narrator: Now complete the steps in your book.

Narrator: Chapter 8, Controlling Crime
Page 118
Listening for main ideas, Step 1

Interviewer: Amy, because you're a lawyer, I wanted to get your opinion about crime control. And what I'd like to know is . . . what do you think really works . . . not for hardened criminals, but for first-time offenders?

Amy: Well, you're asking me a pretty complex question. The first step, of course, is deterrence – to stop people from committing crime in the first place. That involves the economy – are there enough jobs for everyone? There should be. And the social structure – are there enough support systems? And so on.

Interviewer: And what about when people are convicted and put in prison?

Amy: Then the goal should be to have rehabilitation programs *inside* prisons, so that when the person comes *out*, they don't return to a life of crime. The problem is that recently, the kinds of programs that existed in the past – like education programs and drug treatment programs – have been cut. And so, convicted criminals are *not* being rehabilitated.

Interviewer: Can you explain a little more about these education programs and drug programs?

Amy: Yes. In some states, where the drug laws are very harsh, you end up having a lot of people in prisons who are not the kingpins of drug deals, but who are actually drug addicts. The point is that they need help. That's why there need to be programs that have a psychological component, and an educational component. Because without these programs, people don't become rehabilitated. The prisoners have a lot of time on their hands, and a culture develops inside the prison. It takes on a life of its own, and gangs start. You see, gangs provide a family away from home. But we need to make prison a less repressive experience. Then we also need bridge programs.

Interviewer: Bridge programs?

Amy: Yes, for when they come *out* of prison. What is clear statistically is that most criminals are recidivists. That means they are repeat offenders. People go into prison, get out, and go right back in again. Bridge programs help with housing and jobs, so that society doesn't look at released prisoners in such a disdainful way, and so that no stigma is attached to them once they reenter society. But, unfortunately, there are only a very small number of these programs.

Narrator: Now complete the steps in your book.

Narrator: Chapter 8, Controlling Crime
Page 121
Note taking: Recording numerical information, Step 2

Jonathan Stack: In 1972, the U.S. Supreme Court ruled that capital punishment was unconstitutional, but the Court reinstated it in 1976.

Since then, about six hundred executions have been carried out.

Student: I read that according to recent statistics, sixty-seven percent of Americans favor the death penalty in cases of murder. That's two-thirds of the population!

Jonathan Stack: In the United States, there are about nine murders a year per one hundred thousand people. In Japan, for example, that figure is 0.5. In France, it's 1.1.

Narrator: Now complete the steps in your book.

Narrator: Chapter 8, Controlling Crime
Page 123
Note taking: Using your notes to ask questions and make comments, Step 1

Jonathan Stack: There is probably no issue in criminal justice today more controversial than capital punishment – the death penalty. As you probably know, the United States is the only Western industrialized nation that allows capital punishment. In 1972, the U.S. Supreme Court ruled that capital punishment was unconstitutional, but the Court reinstated it in 1976. Since then, about six hundred executions have been carried out. Executions are usually carried out by lethal injection or electrocution. Today, I'd like to talk to you about some of the main arguments against this form of punishment.

Of course, the first question most people ask is: Does capital punishment deter crime? Well, although there are studies that have linked the increase in executions with a decrease in homicides, a great many social scientists argue that there is no such link. In fact, states with the most executions are also the states with the highest homicide rates. So I do not believe that it is an effective deterrence. The death penalty does not deter murder.

My second point is that capital punishment is not used fairly. Nearly all prisoners who are sentenced to death are poor males. And some states, like Louisiana and Mississippi, still use the death penalty, whereas other states, like Iowa, do not. Race is also a factor. Historically, African-Americans have been more likely to be executed than whites, both in proportion to the general population and to the prison population.

I have another major objection to capital punishment, which is that because we are human, there is always the possibility that we can make mistakes. We always have to question if we have gotten the facts right. According to the Death Penalty Information Center in Washington, at least ninety-six prisoners were recently released from death row in twenty-two states because they were improperly convicted or because evidence of their innocence was discovered after they were sentenced to death. In the state of Illinois a few years ago, there were twenty-six people on death row, and thirteen of them were released, because new evidence proved that they were innocent. These are thirteen people who would have been executed by the state. So in other words, we do make mistakes, and we have to allow for the possibility of that error.

Once you execute somebody, you've done something that should not be in the domain of the state. It's almost as if you're playing the role of God on life or death issues. I believe that killing someone is a moral decision, and that it is not a decision the state should make.

Narrator: Now complete the steps in your book.

Jonathan Stack: Now I'll take some questions.

Student: Yes, I have a question. Isn't it true that the public supports the death penalty? I read that according to recent statistics, sixty-seven percent of Americans favor the death penalty in cases of murder. That's two-thirds of the population!

Jonathan Stack: It's true that there is support for the death penalty, but it is also true that people's moods and opinions are difficult to understand through statistics. I think this figure might reflect people's concern about violent crime in general. The United States is by far the most violent industrialized nation. In the United States, there are about nine murders a year per one hundred thousand people. In Japan, for example, that figure is 0.5. In France, it's 1.1. So Americans are understandably concerned about violence.

Student: Excuse me, Mr. Stack. What did you say the figure was in the United States?

Jonathan Stack: It's about nine murders per year, per one hundred thousand people.

Student: I'd like to make a comment. I mean, if someone commits a really bad crime, don't they deserve to be punished just as severely?

Jonathan Stack: The problem with the death penalty is that on an emotional level, you can understand why people want it. If you've suffered the loss of a loved one, your immediate response is to want revenge; it's a normal, natural reaction. But I feel that the reason we have laws is that they allow us to rise above our personal, emotional response to crime. This form of retribution is not the answer. The idea of having laws in a society is that together – as a society – we are stronger than the sum of our parts. We can rise above our personal, emotional response to crime. The legal system is supposed to elevate us: it is set up so that it is better than us. Individually, we are flawed, but as a society we are strong.

Student: I thought it was interesting what you said about the death penalty not being fair, because it was applied to some people but not to others. Could you talk a little bit more about that?

Jonathan Stack: Yes. In many ways, capital punishment is very arbitrary. If you really believed in the death penalty as a principle, as a punishment for a horrific crime, then every single person who has committed this crime would have to be executed. But that would mean that we would have about fifty thousand executions a year. That's absurd. Nobody would stand for that. It would mean that the state was some kind of killing machine. The fact is that we do execute some people, but other people who have committed similar crimes are not executed. So the death penalty is not applied equally to all people.

Student: Mr. Stack, I'd like to thank you for your comments today. I'm opposed to the death penalty myself, and I don't think we talk enough about these issues.

Jonathan Stack: I'm pleased to come. Thank you.

Narrator: Now complete the steps in your book.

9

Narrator: Chapter 9, Cultural Change
Page 129
Recording numerical information, Step 2

Man: Today's computer has its origins in the distant past. The abacus, a tool for counting, goes back to 500 B.C., when it was in common use. But it was not until many centuries later, in 1642, that Pascal invented the first calculating machine.

It was not until several centuries after that, in 1938, that the first computing machine was built that used a binary method of operation – the zeros and ones that are the basis of much of today's technology. And in 1956 the term "artificial intelligence" was first used.

A computer with a keyboard and monitor appeared around 1960. The mouse was invented as a time-saving device for giving commands to a computer in 1968.

In 1975, the first personal computer was marketed. And the first widely used laptop computer appeared in 1985.

In 1997, "Deep Blue," a supercomputer, beat the world chess champion in a six-game match. By that same year – 1997 – there was a computer called a teraflop that could perform one trillion operations per second.

Narrator: Now complete the steps in your book.

Narrator: Chapter 9, Cultural Change
Page 131
Listening for opinions, Step 2

Interviewer: Nina, I'd like to get your opinion on computers. You know, your thoughts about them.

Nina: Well, first, I think the amount of information that's available to us is absolutely overwhelming. It's much more than people can really take advantage of, and the idea that it will improve our life in some way is not really true. A lot of people don't even have access to computers. So it can't really help them.

Interviewer: OK, but if you *do* have a computer, does it help you?

Nina: Mmm . . . not sure. It's fun to spend hours a day surfing the net, investigating something that interests you, but then you sorta get lost, click here, click here, click here, click here . . . and five hours later, you realize that you haven't seen your family today, and you've been sitting there chasing down all this information that you think is so important. And yeah, it's wonderful on one hand to have the Internet at your disposal, but there's a way that books just bring knowledge alive to you in a completely different way. You get to discuss books with your friends, to share ideas

with others, but all people talk about when they're discussing the Internet is how much time they wasted.

Interviewer: Yeah, and how annoying those pop-up ads are!

Nina: Well, that's another thing. When you turn it on, you have to close the home shopping network that pops up onto your screen . . . and some people can't be left alone with that.

Interviewer: Like who?

Nina: Like my husband. If they say on the ad: This will do this and this, he's like "Oh! This will be great, it does this and this!" And he clicks and then a few days later, a package arrives. At our house. He bought a scanner and we can't get it to work. And, oh yeah, an electronic protector that is incompatible with our system. It's frightening. I know a little bit about the Internet, but I usually can't find anything I want.

Interviewer: Well, what about computers in general?

Nina: Well in order to understand how much your hard drive can hold, you have to read some book that's about an inch thick. Oh, and they shut down for no apparent reason. They freeze and shut down, and you don't know what happened and you have to call some special service – it's just a waste of time. And I'd prefer to spend my time in other ways.

Interviewer: So you don't think that modern technology helps our personal relationships, do you?

Nina: Well, it's interesting. One thing that I like, actually, is e-mail. I write short messages just to stay in touch with people. And I wouldn't do that if I had to sit down and write a letter, and look up their address, and find a stamp, and put it in an envelope, and take it to the post office, and remember to mail it. So I really like e-mail, but I also think it becomes an easy way to feel like we've had contact with people, when really you haven't had any contact. Or very little. I mean, you toss out some news, but there's been no direct communication. But letters are different. People save them because they were particularly meaningful or remind you of a particular time in your life. And you can look at 'em years later. You don't have that with e-mail. It's there and it's gone.

Interviewer: That's very true.

Nina: And don't forget that computers were touted as a way to get toward the paperless society. We were gonna use less paper – or *no* paper – and we were gonna save all these trees, but because the computer systems are always shutting down, and going wrong, you've got to have a backup system, um, so to me it almost seems like a trick. Computers might be great for writing and editing things, and everything comes out looking great and all that, but they don't save paper! So in that sense I think they were misrepresented.

Interviewer: Well, do you think that kids feel differently about technology?

Nina: Yeah, I do. 'Cause they've been raised on it. They take it for granted. They learn it when they're young and they're not intimidated. And they've been playing those games where you shoot down those ugly little faces for so long that they know what they're looking for. So, I think they make better use of it than the average, you know, forty-year-old.

Narrator: Now complete the steps in your book.

**Narrator: Chapter 9, Cultural Change
Page 132
Answering true/false questions, Step 2**

Interviewer: Hi, Kelly. You're twenty now, right?

Kelly: Right.

Interviewer: What do *you* think about what Nina said?

Kelly: I definitely agree that younger people are less intimidated by technology. But when I compare myself with other people my age, I don't see myself as particularly good with computers – most of my friends are much

better with computers than I am. But this summer, I worked in an office with lots of adults, and I realized that I'm a lot more comfortable with technology than they are.

Interviewer: Do you use e-mail a lot?

Kelly: Well, I *do* see Nina's point that letters make better keepsakes, but e-mail's just so much more convenient! For example, I'm away at college now and I don't know how I could keep in touch with my high school friends without e-mail. I like e-mail because it's such a casual form of communication, it's great for just saying hello and checking up on people. For more extended interaction, I still use the phone a lot. But for just telling people that you thought of them that day or that you miss them e-mail is great.

Interviewer: How often would you say that you e-mail people?

Kelly: Well, I check my e-mail at least five times a day, I would estimate. Actually, probably a bit more. I also have IM configured so that it loads the program automatically whenever I turn on my computer, so I am on that a lot as well. It definitely makes you spend more time on the computer than you meant to. Sometimes I just turn on my computer to check on one little thing, and all of a sudden three people send me instant messages and I talk to them for half an hour. But it's not wasted time, because I love to hear from my friends.

Interviewer: So young people are better with computers than adults.

Kelly: I don't know if kids are really better at computers or just more used to them. Computers can definitely be intimidating, especially when they go wrong. For people who aren't familiar with them, I think a typical response is to use them as little as possible. My dad is like that. But once you get over your initial fear of just fiddling around with them and testing things out, it becomes a lot more fun, and it's really not difficult.

Interviewer: What about your friends?

Kelly: Well, I guess my generation is hooked on the Internet. But people don't make it their whole life, it's just one other thing they like to do. It really opens up a lot of doors, the Internet. It makes a lot of things accessible. My college now is a pretty web-based school. At first I was a little bit surprised at how much the Internet was used. Like for example, all of my syllabi for my classes are online.

Interviewer: Do you think the Internet has any disadvantages?

Kelly: Well, something that is bad about the Internet is that not everyone has access to it. I feel like, when my generation is grown up and part of the work force, computer skills are just going to be assumed, they won't be an added asset like I think they are today. So what will happen to the people in my generation who don't have these computer skills, you know? They're really going to be at a disadvantage. So, I think the Internet could increase the disparities between different classes, which is horrible. Or maybe technology just illuminates existing disparities in a different way. I'm not sure. In my own life though, I love having the Internet. I don't know what I'd do without it!

Narrator: Now complete the steps in your book.

Narrator: Chapter 9, Cultural Change
Page 136
Note taking: Listening for stress and intonation, Step 2

Narrator: One.

Graciano E. Matos: Well, what are the skills that you need?

Narrator: Two.

Graciano E. Matos: Then you decided where you were going to apply, put your resume with a cover letter in a stamped envelope, and waited anxiously for someone to get back to you.

Narrator: Three.

Graciano E. Matos: In fact, technology has not so much changed the process as enhanced it.

Narrator: Four.

Graciano E. Matos: You can research employment not just in your city, but also in your state, your region, your country, and even other countries.

Narrator: Five.

Graciano E. Matos: In addition to using newspapers and the phone, the Internet has become the tool of preference for getting more details on job openings, applications, and other necessary information.

Narrator: Now complete the steps in your book.

Narrator: Chapter 9, Cultural Change
Page 137
Note taking: Listening for stress and intonation, Step 1

Graciano E. Matos: Good afternoon, everybody. My name is Graciano E. Matos. I'm a career counselor, and students often approach me with concerns about their future. You see, we are living in a society of great technological change, and the skills you need now are different from the ones you needed in the past. With the presence of fax machines, advanced telecommunications systems, industrial technology, and the Internet, the process of getting a job in today's world and the skills necessary to be successful in your job have changed for the majority of the U.S. population. And although you still need all of the old skills, you also need the new ones.

Well, what are the skills that you need? How can you use new technologies to help you? First, let's look at how you find a job. The traditional method of hunting for a job in the past required first, doing research on jobs that were available in your field, typically by looking in newspapers, TV ads, and making phone calls to prospective employers. Then you decided where you were going to apply, put your resume with a cover letter in a stamped envelope, and waited anxiously for someone to get back to you.

Well, today, maybe the job search and application process are very much the same, but the tools used are much more advanced, and they require more skills and expertise. In fact, technology has not so much changed the process as enhanced it. The benefit, both for the employer and the employee, is that this makes the search more open to people of different socioeconomic backgrounds from all over the world. But as more people are involved, it becomes more competitive for the applicant than it ever was before.

The secret to preparing yourself for the working world today is learning these new and ever changing tools and combining them with the older methods people have been using for years.

For example, the Internet. The Internet should be used as a giant newspaper in which the pages are constantly changing. You can research employment not just in your city, but also in your state, your region, your country, and even other countries.

In addition to using newspapers and the phone, the Internet has become the tool of preference for getting more details on job openings, applications, and other necessary information. In the past you might have had a . . . a desk full of newspaper ads just to keep track of where you should apply. But now you can copy information from a web page and paste it into a Microsoft Word document that's easy to access and print anytime. In many ways, it's easier now: You don't have to worry about paying for a stamp and walking to the nearest post office! Just type your job application, click, and send it through e-mail; it gets there in an instant.

Narrator: Now complete the steps in your book.

**Narrator: Chapter 9, Cultural Change
Page 138
Note taking: Using your notes to answer test questions, Step 2**

Graciano E. Matos: So, the procedures for finding a job and sending an application have changed quite a lot.

Now let's talk about actually getting the job. You need to be able to participate well in an interview because in most jobs, you will need to interact with colleagues and clients – not only face to face, but in telephone conversations, too. You will need to express yourself well and have excellent control of what you want to say and how to say it. These skills are needed more than ever in today's high-pressure world.

Each company where you have an interview will expect you to know something about the work they do and have intelligent questions and comments during the interview. And when they hire you, you'll be expected to complete multiple tasks, and be willing to move around and work in different areas of the company.

Of course, there are also certain technological skills that are expected of people today. Every situation is unique but let's take as an example a position in an office environment. This type of position requires basic to advanced knowledge of computer applications. You have to know how to write a simple but professional looking letter, and you have to know how to put together a presentation in Microsoft PowerPoint with basic effects and organize data in a spreadsheet program. Advanced users should know how to create and organize a database. If you are looking for any type of administrative work you can forget about the good old days of paper calendars, rolodexes, and file cabinets. Now, we have links to digital databases that store all the information that used to be kept on paper such as appointments, clients' records, and other important information. Many departments use spreadsheet programs to keep track of all transactions, costs, and profits. These programs are essential to an organization's survival as well as your career's survival.

Let's continue with our basic example of a typical job in an office. Now that you know about the skills necessary to be productive in the office of the twenty-first century, you must have a plan for how to acquire these skills. The first thing you should have in mind is that in the same manner that technology has become a vital part of a modern organization's life, it should also become part of yours. Whenever given a chance you should enhance your keyboard skills. E-mail your friends. Practice with PowerPoint. Try making simple posters to announce an event, like a-a party or some activity that you and your friends will do together. You can even practice with pre-made databases by storing telephone numbers and addresses. The best advice I can give anyone is to play with the computer in your free time and become familiar with its operating system, software, and hardware. Try to figure out what each program does and how to use it to your benefit. A computer class on the level of your expertise is also recommended to perfect those skills you learned on your own. Learning more advanced functions is highly recommended as well. It's easy to look through books and-and free tutorials found on the Internet. Even novice users can learn how to create professional looking flyers, business cards, and other documents you will need in the workplace.

This is the advice I give to the students I counsel, and I hope it's been helpful for you.

Narrator: Now complete the steps in your book.

**Narrator: Chapter 10, Global Issues
Page 142
Personalizing the topic, Step 2**

Narrator: One.
[*birds singing*]

Narrator: Two.
[*car horn honking*]

Narrator: Three.
[*subway*]

Narrator: Four.
[*music from a boom box*]

Narrator: Five.
[*heavy traffic*]

Narrator: Six.
[*shopping mall*]

Narrator: Seven.
[*bubbling brook*]

Narrator: Eight.
[*musical concert in a concert hall*]

Narrator: Nine.
[*people arguing over a parking spot*]

Narrator: Ten.
[*dogs barking*]

Narrator: Now complete the steps in your book.

**Narrator: Chapter 10, Global Issues
Page 144
Retelling what you have heard, Step 2**

Interviewer: Barbara, what's interesting to you about living in the city? Why do you like it?

Barbara: Well, I'm just a city girl! One time I bought a house in the country to escape from the urban ills, and then found myself totally bored with country life, because you have to drive everywhere and there's not much to do. I'm used to the fast pace of the city. There's a whole variety of museums, movies, coffee shops, and places to interact with people. But sitting alone in the country, ugh – you know, unless you like to grow, or garden. Or putter around and build things with your hands.

Interviewer: OK, but what about for vacation? I mean lots of city people rent vacation houses in the country.

Barbara: But to me, going to the country for a vacation makes no sense at all. There's so much work to do. First you have to get there, and then . . . I don't know, I think I can relax better in the city. Besides, the country has bugs. There you are supposedly enjoying yourself, in the fresh country air, but you're being eaten alive by a variety of different bugs. You can't enjoy yourself. You're being stung and eaten to death. You can't relax. Let's put it this way, if you like boredom, you'll like the country. People who like a lot of stimulation, you know, can't hack it. And then there's the transportation thing. I mean, to get a carton of milk you have to drive three miles. So the whole car culture thing kicks in. Give me the city anytime!

Interviewer: Well, what would you say is the one thing you like *most* about the city?

Barbara: The interactive social life. People get together. I like it when you call up and people say, come on over, and you hang out together, and it's just fun.

Interviewer: Yeah, and what about the suburbs?

Barbara: Well, that's even more hateful than the country to me.

Interviewer: Why?

Barbara: Well, the suburbs don't even have any of the good country air. There's nothing to do. You're just stuck there. And for young people, there are all sorts of problems – alcohol, drugs, you have to drive everywhere. Look, I go to my friend's house in the suburbs. Do you ever see anyone walking in the street? No. It's totally zero. There's nothing going on. What can I say, you know? It's not for me. I do have one or two suburban friends who like it, because they make a barbecue, and the birds are chirping . . . but not me!

Oh, and then there's another thing I really hate. In the city, you can make mistakes, but you always get a second chance. But in the country and the suburbs, you're labeled, you feel like wow, that's it, you're labeled. And that label doesn't come off easily.

Interviewer: Well, do you think the city is lonely? Or dangerous?

Barbara: No! In the city people live in little communities. They have interactive social lives. And I don't think the city is particularly dangerous.

Narrator: Now complete the steps in your book.

Narrator: Chapter 10, Global Issues
Page 145
Listening for details, Step 2

Interviewer: Can you tell me about the different places you've lived, Kenny?

Kenny: I grew up in a big city, New York, but I always thought I would want to live somewhere else.

Interviewer: And did you move?

Kenny: I did. What finally drove me out of New York was the traffic. I felt stuck in the city, like I was trapped. I'd always spent summers in the country – in Maine, in the woods, on a lake, and I felt free there, but I wasn't ready to be in the country full time, so for the next seven years we lived in a small town.

Interviewer: And was that better?

Kenny: No, I never liked it. I moved back to New York because of my kids. I didn't want them cheering for different sports teams!

Interviewer: Do you feel better about life in the city now?

Kenny: Well, I have my ups and downs. What bothers me most about the urban lifestyle is still the traffic. And the parking. Here's an example for you. One time my mother was dropping my daughter off after taking her to a play. This is just a law-abiding grandmother doing what normal grandmothers love to do, hanging out with her grandchildren and taking her to a show.

OK, so she comes to drop my daughter off and of course there's no parking. My mother is seventy-five, and she needs a little break, so despite not having a legal parking spot, she steps inside the house before driving another forty-five minutes home. She was in the house five minutes, and it cost her fifty dollars! She got a parking ticket! I mean, taking a grandchild to a show doesn't cause stress in the suburbs. But in the big city it's a big deal.

Interviewer: How does your wife feel?

Kenny: Well, for my wife, it's the dirt that bothers her.

Interviewer: Doesn't that bother you, too?

Kenny: No, I don't really mind the dirt – I suppose I'm used to it. Other people complain about graffiti, but that doesn't really bother me, either.

Interviewer: So, on the whole, would you say you prefer city living to other places?

Kenny: Well, the thing is I like *big* cities, I also like wild, remote places in the country. I don't like anything in between, like small cities or suburbs. I think small towns are the worst. I mean, if you're gonna have a lot of buildings and cars, at least you should have a lot of interesting people. People are the best part of cities. If you're not gonna have people on the streets, then please give me some trees, streams, boulders, animals.

Interviewer: Well, besides the interesting people, is there any other thing you like about the city?

Kenny: I know it's weird, but I especially love the city on gray drizzly days.

Interviewer: You do?

Kenny: Yeah. It's beautiful how the gray of the buildings blends in with the gray of the sky. But on bright sunny days I hate it. I want to be on a mountain, hiking in the woods, something like that. But because of the traffic, I don't go anywhere except the park usually. It's frustrating on those sunny days. So I can only be truly happy in the city when the weather is bad.

Interviewer: So what's your idea of the ideal place to live?

Kenny: The ideal place to live would be a big city that ends suddenly, and then right away you're in a rural area. So on rainy days I'd stay home and watch the rain, and on sunny days I'd go mountain climbing. And at night, I'd have a choice: I could camp out and cook burgers or go home and order Chinese take-out.

Narrator: Now complete the steps in your book.

**Narrator: Chapter 10, Global Issues
Page 151
Note taking: Using handouts to help you take notes, Step 1**

Narrator: Excerpt from Part One of the lecture, Handout 1

Bryan Gilroy: I'd like you to take a look at the first handout, which is part of a classic study published by Ebenezer Howard a century ago. It shows three magnets, representing what he calls "town," "country," and "town-country." You'll see immediately that he lists pros and cons for each environment. For example, the country has "beauty of nature" but "long hours and low wages." The town has "social opportunity" but "isolation." What's interesting about "The Three Magnets" is that although it was written in 1898, it identifies many of the same reasons that people are still being pulled away from rural areas and into urban or suburban environments.

Narrator: Excerpt from Part Two of the lecture, Handout 2

Bryan Gilroy: Cities are also changing shape in other ways. Look at handout 2. The Concentric Zone Model represents the structure of some cities built at the beginning of the twentieth century. The business district is in the center, surrounded by the other zones. But the Sector Model and the Multiple Nuclei Model are probably more typical of the cities we know today. They show the urban sprawl that's occurring in contemporary cities. Urban sprawl basically means that cities are spreading out, often in an uncontrolled way. Notice that in these two models the business district is close to all the other districts.

Narrator: Now complete the steps in your book.

Narrator: Chapter 10, Global Issues
Page 152
Note taking: Combining the skills, Step 1

Bryan Gilroy: Good morning and welcome to today's lecture. Today we're going to discuss the mass urbanization of the world's population, which is an unprecedented trend worldwide. I'd like you to take a look at the first handout, which is part of a classic study published by Ebenezer Howard a century ago. It shows three magnets, representing what he calls "town," "country," and "town-country." You'll see immediately that he lists pros and cons for each environment. For example, the country has "beauty of nature" but "long hours and low wages." The town has "social opportunity" but "isolation." What's interesting about "The Three Magnets" is that although it was written in 1898, it identifies many of the same reasons that people are still being pulled away from rural areas and into urban or suburban environments. In this lecture, I'll focus on two major reasons why people are moving to cities.

Well, the first reason is economic. People are moving to the cities because that's where they can find jobs and earn money. Until the twentieth century, the major source of employment, full and part time, was farming. However, the need for people to work on the land gets less and less as we are able to do more and more things by machine. Now, no more than fifteen percent of all jobs are connected to farming. Jobs now are being created in information technology, manufacturing and service areas, such as tourism and financing. And all of these new jobs are in or around major cities.

The second reason for the move to cities has to do with quality of life issues – comfort and convenience. For example, most of us would like our children to receive a good education, and cities often offer better schools. And then for many, city life is just more comfortable. There are transportation networks, shops, and places of entertainment. An interesting consequence of urbanization is that the average age of people in the countryside is increasing, while that of the cities is falling. More old people stay in the countryside than young people and the opposite is true in the cities. This is of course connected to the fact that it's the young people who want jobs.

Narrator: Now complete the steps in your book.

Narrator: Chapter 10, Global Issues
Page 154
Note taking: Combining the skills, Step 1

Bryan Gilroy: Now I'd like to identify three key changes in our cities. First of all, they're getting bigger and bigger. For the first time in history, there will soon be more people living in urban areas than in rural environments. Think about that for a minute. Most cities are bigger now than ever before. Tokyo, Mexico, Bombay, São Paulo are among the largest cities in the world, and each of these cities will soon have approximately twenty million people. In 1950, New York City was the only city with a population of ten million. For the first time in the history of society, we now have many cities with populations of over ten million people – what we call *megacities*. Tokyo, Mexico, Bombay, and São Paulo are just a few examples of today's megacities. And experts say that the number of megacities will increase in the future.

Cities are not just getting bigger: they're also changing shape. They're getting taller, because land is getting more and more expensive. So instead of having a few big houses on a piece of land, we can have a tall apartment building that a thousand people can live in. All of you can probably think of buildings or parks or stores that have been torn down to make room for bigger, taller, or more modern buildings. Skyscrapers have become a symbol of modern cities, like the recently constructed Taipei 101 Tower in Taiwan. Now it's the tallest building in the world – 1,674 feet high.

Cities are also changing shape in other ways. Look at handout 2. The Concentric Zone Model represents the structure of some cities built at the beginning of the twentieth century. The business district is in the center, surrounded by the other zones. But the Sector Model and the Multiple Nuclei Model are probably more typical of the cities we know today. They show the urban sprawl that's occurring in contemporary cities. Urban sprawl basically means that cities are spreading out, often in an uncontrolled way. Notice that in these two models the business district is close to all the other districts. Another change in the shape of cities is that cities now tend to become linked to each other, like Osaka-Kobe-Kyoto, in Japan, which has a huge combined population. This sprawl often occurs in random and unpredictable ways and has a huge impact on the quality of life of city residents.

The third change is that our cities are breaking up into smaller communities, often by ethnic group or income level. Of course, many cities do have a kind of identity or personality, but a city is not homogeneous. For example, migrants to the cities often want to live in their own communities or with people from a similar cultural background. Another example is that if you are moving from a smaller community to a city, you will be most likely to move close to friends or family members, who will help you get a job or give you support. However, this often means that people stay within their community and do not come into contact with others from different backgrounds.

How will cities continue to change in the future? Well, we can predict that cities will continue to grow in the future. The biggest challenge facing us now is to improve the quality of life in cities, because sadly, they don't always offer the economic security, the safety, or the comfort they promise. Many cities have slum areas or ghettos, where people live in dangerous or destitute conditions. The beautiful architecture and vibrant nightlife are one face of the city. But cities also have problems of inequality, crowding, and poverty.

Narrator: Now complete the steps in your book.

Lecture Quizzes
and Quiz Answers

Chapter **1** LECTURE QUIZ

Answer the following questions on Parts One and Two of the Chapter 1 lecture, *Family Lessons*. Use only your lecture notes to help you. Answer each question as fully as possible. You will receive 20 points for each complete and correct answer.

1 List three common ways that children acquire good behavior within a family setting. Give examples of each one. (20 points)

2 Explain why both rewards and punishments are considered controversial. (20 points)

3 Who are a child's role models? Why are they important? (20 points)

4 Why are parents often worried about the lessons children learn from others? (20 points)

5 What is the most important thing in a child's environment? (20 points)

Name _____   Date _____

Chapter **2** LECTURE QUIZ

Answer the following questions on Parts One and Two of the Chapter 2 lecture, *Culture Shock – Group Pressure in Action.* Use only your lecture notes to help you. Answer each question as fully as possible. You will receive 20 points for each complete and correct answer.

1 Define *culture shock,* and explain why it is an example of group pressure. (20 points)

2 Explain how a person can react and feel when they go to another country and experience a different set of social rules. (20 points)

3 What are the three main stages of culture shock, and which emotions tend to accompany each stage? (20 points)

4 Tourists often suffer from culture shock. What are some other situations in which people suffer from culture shock? (20 points)

5 Why is it important that we try to learn about other cultures? (20 points)

Chapter **3** LECTURE QUIZ

Answer the following questions on Parts One and Two of the Chapter 3 lecture, *The Benefits of Single-Sex Education for Girls.* Use only your lecture notes to help you. Answer each question as fully as possible. You will receive 20 points for each complete and correct answer.

1 What is single-sex education? (20 points)

2 Explain three of the main arguments against single-sex education. (20 points)

3 What are some ways in which girls learn differently from boys? (20 points)

4 How does a single-sex environment help girls to develop self-confidence? (20 points)

5 How can the feeling of self-confidence help young women in the adult world? (20 points)

Chapter 4 LECTURE QUIZ

Answer the following questions on Parts One and Two of the Chapter 4 lecture, *Gender and Language*. Use only your lecture notes to help you. Answer each question as fully as possible. You will receive 20 points for each complete and correct answer.

1 Why are the terms "Miss" and "Mrs." examples of sexist language? Why is the term "Mr." not sexist? What nonsexist term can be used instead of "Miss" or "Mrs."? (20 points)

2 What is the difference between gender-specific terms and gender-neutral terms? Give two examples. (20 points)

3 Explain why we should use gender-neutral language. (20 points)

4 What problems occur in English with vocabulary and grammar when using gender-neutral language? (20 points)

5 Give an example of how the language we use can affect the way we think. (20 points)

Chapter **5** LECTURE QUIZ

Answer the following questions on Parts One and Two of the Chapter 5 lecture, *From Event to Story – Making It to the News*. Use only your lecture notes to help you. Answer each question as fully as possible. You will receive 20 points for each complete and correct answer.

1 What different kinds of journalists are there? Why are some journalists called "reporters"? (20 points)

2 What are some steps involved in preparing a news story? (20 points)

3 What important questions do readers want answered at the beginning of every story? (20 points)

4 Why do newspapers try so hard to make sure that the stories they publish are accurate? (20 points)

5 What are three main elements of a good news story? (20 points)

Chapter 6 LECTURE QUIZ

Answer the following questions on Parts One and Two of the Chapter 6 lecture, *Dangers of the Mass Media*. Use only your lecture notes to help you. Answer each question as fully as possible. You will receive 20 points for each complete and correct answer.

1 What does the term *mass media* include? (20 points)

2 What evidence exists to suggest that TV can make us violent? (20 points)

3 What forms of mass media can encourage us to be passive? What forms of mass media can be addictive? Explain. (20 points)

4 What is *product placement*? Give examples. (20 points)

5 How can the media invade our privacy? (20 points)

Chapter **7** LECTURE QUIZ

Answer the following questions on Parts One and Two of the Chapter 7 lecture, *Crime and Ways of Solving Crime*. Use only your lecture notes to help you. Answer each question as fully as possible. You will receive 20 points for each complete and correct answer.

1 Name two categories of crime. Give two examples of types of crime in each of the two categories. (20 points)

2 Explain what is meant by *white-collar crime* and give two examples of it. (20 points)

3 Why is corporate crime difficult to prosecute. Give an example of a corporate crime that was successfully prosecuted. (20 points)

4 Explain what is meant by *interrogation, crime hotlines,* and *fingerprinting*. (20 points)

5 When was DNA first used to solve a crime? How accurate is it? (20 points)

Chapter 8 LECTURE QUIZ

Answer the following questions on Parts One and Two of the Chapter 8 lecture, *The Death Penalty.* Use only your lecture notes to help you. Answer each question as fully as possible. You will receive 20 points for each complete and correct answer.

1 Which industrialized countries in the Western world use capital punishment? What is the history of capital punishment in the United States? (20 points)

2 Why do many people argue that the death penalty does not deter crime? (20 points)

3 Why do some people think that the death penalty is an arbitrary punishment? (20 points)

4 Explain the issues about violent crime in the United States as presented in the lecture. (20 points)

5 Explain the lecturer's opinion about the purpose of having laws and a legal system. (20 points)

Chapter 9 LECTURE QUIZ

Answer the following questions on Parts One and Two of the Chapter 9 lecture, *Basic Work Skills Necessary in the Twenty-first Century*. Use only your lecture notes to help you. Answer each question as fully as possible. You will receive 20 points for each complete and correct answer.

1 What were the traditional methods of job hunting? (20 points)

2 Explain how job hunting has been enhanced by technology. (20 points)

3 Which traditional skills are still necessary? (20 points)

4 Explain how the office environment today is different from the past. (20 points)

5 How can you practice on the computer to help yourself improve your computer skills? (20 points)

Chapter 10 Lecture Quiz

Answer the following questions on Parts One and Two of the Chapter 10 lecture, *Our Changing Cities*. Use only the lecture notes and the handouts to help you. Answer each question as fully as possible. You will receive 20 points for each complete and correct answer.

1 What is happening to the world's population today? (20 points)

2 What are two main reasons why people are moving to urban environments? (20 points)

3 Explain three ways in which cities are changing shape. (20 points)

4 Explain how the Sector Model and the Multiple Nuclei Model (in Handout 2) show urban sprawl. How is the position of the Central Business District in these two models different from its position in the Concentric Zone Model? (20 points)

5 Why do cities often break up into smaller communities? Give two examples. (20 points)

Lecture Quiz Answers

Chapter 1 LECTURE QUIZ ANSWERS

1 Children learn good behavior through rewards, punishments, and modeling. An example of a reward is giving children ice cream after they eat their vegetables. An example of a punishment is not allowing children to go out and play because they got a bad grade on a homework assignment. Modeling is when children copy their parents' good behavior. An example of modeling is when a parent studies with a child.

2 Rewards and punishments are controversial because many people think they are not effective or necessary. Sometimes rewards are like bribes and do not teach children to be responsible. Physical punishment, in particular, is extremely controversial. Opponents argue it doesn't teach children anything and may encourage them to be violent.

3 A child's role models include parents, other family members, friends, babysitters, and teachers.

4 Parents worry that their children may learn bad behavior from other children and from TV because it can be extremely violent.

5 The most important thing for children is to be raised in an environment where the rules are fair and consistent, and where the child is loved and exposed to strong, positive role models.

Chapter 2 LECTURE QUIZ ANSWERS

1 *Culture shock* is the term used to describe the experience many people have when they go to another country. It is an example of group pressure because it occurs when you are surrounded by people who follow different rules of behavior.

2 People experiencing culture shock often feel in a state of shock, as if a bucket of cold water has been thrown over them. They can act irrationally because they feel out of control.

3 The first stage has been called the "honeymoon" stage and includes positive feelings of happiness and excitement. This stage is followed by the "letdown," when feelings change and people experience loneliness and confusion. Finally, during the "resignation" stage, they become adjusted to their new environment.

4 In addition to tourists, immigrants often experience culture shock. Also, older residents of a country that has many new immigrants may experience culture shock because they may feel that they are surrounded by people who practice customs different from their own.

5 It is important that we learn about other cultures because in today's world people from many cultures often live in close contact. If we understand other cultures, it will help us to avoid tense relationships that may come from this close contact.

Chapter 3 LECTURE QUIZ ANSWERS

1 Single-sex education means that girls and boys are separated and taught in different schools.

2 The lecturer mentions three main arguments against single-sex education. The first is that it is old-fashioned and appears to go against the aims and goals of feminists and liberal educators, which is to provide fairness. The second is that in a single-sex environment, girls do not develop the ability to be comfortable and competitive around boys. The third is that a single-sex environment does not provide a smooth transition into the "real world" of adult men and women.

3 Girls can often concentrate on higher-level, abstract thinking at an earlier age than boys. They work for longer periods of time, and they enjoy collaborative activities. Finally, they are kind and cooperative, rather than competitive.

4 Single-sex environments allow girls to develop self-confidence because they do not have the distraction and different learning styles of boys.

5 Self-confidence allows girls to enter the adult world of men and women and challenge the rules.

Chapter 4 LECTURE QUIZ ANSWERS

1 The terms "Miss" and "Mrs." are sexist because they reveal whether a woman is married, as opposed to the term "Mr.," which does not reveal whether a man is married. The term "Ms." has become common and allows the problem to be avoided.

2 A gender-specific term implies that all people identified by that term must be one gender. For example, the implication is that a *mailman* or a *policeman* must be male. Gender-neutral terms, such as *mail carrier* or *police officer,* imply that these positions can be held by people of either gender.

3 We should use gender-neutral language because it describes the world the way it really is, a world in which men and women often have the same opportunities. Gender-neutral language also acknowledges equality between men and women.

4 Gender-neutral vocabulary can be problematic because new terms such as *mail carrier* have to gain acceptance. Grammar, specifically pronoun use, is another area that is difficult to use correctly when trying to use gender-neutral language.

5 If children grow up hearing a gender-specific term, they internalize certain impressions about men and women. For example, if children always hear the term *chairman,* they think that position can only be held by a man, which is not true. Changing the way we speak, e.g., using *chair* or *chairperson,* can give us different expectations.

Chapter 5 LECTURE QUIZ ANSWERS

1 There are many different kinds of journalists, such as entertainment journalists, sports journalists, and crime journalists. A reporter is a journalist who "reports" the news.

2 The steps include having good relationships with civic organizations, going to the scene of a story, interviewing witnesses, writing the story, discussing the story with an editor, and checking the facts. A variety of editors are involved with the story: a copyeditor, who checks grammar; a proofreader, who checks typographical errors; a photo editor, who chooses photographs; and the editor-in-chief, who decides on which page the story should appear in the newspaper.

3 Readers want to know: What happened? When did it happen? Where did it happen? Who was involved?

4 Newspapers want to publish accurate stories because if they don't, their reputations will be hurt. They may also be sued for libel.

5 Three main elements of a good story are that it has to be new, it has to be unusual, and it has to concern something interesting that readers want to know about.

Chapter 6 LECTURE QUIZ ANSWERS

1 The term *mass media* includes TV, newspapers, magazines, and the radio, as well as newer technologies such as cable, satellite TV, PDAs, and the Internet.

2 TV might promote violence among children and adolescents. There have been incidents of young people copying violent behavior they see on TV. For example, a TV movie showed a subway booth being set on fire and some kids copied that behavior.

3 TV can encourage us to be passive by turning us into couch potatoes. This passivity can lead to our not distinguishing between fantasy and reality and, therefore, making mistakes about important decisions in our lives. In addition to addiction to TV, we can become addicted to the Internet and waste a lot of time. Cell phones also seem to be very addictive.

4 *Product placement* means that certain products are built into the programs and movies we see on TV. For example, the actors might be seen drinking a particular soft drink or wearing a certain brand of running shoe.

5 Advertisers are getting more and more private information about individuals. For example, when you use a credit card or vist a website, you allow yourself to be tracked, and your behavior to be studied.

Chapter **7** LECTURE QUIZ ANSWERS

1 Two categories of crime are misdemeanors and felonies. Misdemeanors include pickpocketing and fare evasion. Felonies include burglary, robbery, arson, kidnapping, rape, and murder. (Students need only include two examples of each category.)

2 White-collar crime refers to crime committed by salaried employees in businesses and corporations. It includes tax fraud, embezzlement, and corporate crime. (Students need only include two of the examples.)

3 Corporate crime is difficult to prosecute because of the difficulty of proving who is responsible and because the criminals are usually wealthy and powerful. A corporate crime that was successfully prosecuted involved the tobacco industry in the United States. The industry was found guilty of killing thousands of people who smoked cigarettes.

4 Interrogation is questioning by the police of witnesses or other people in connection with a crime. Crime hotlines are systems that allow the public to communicate information to the police anonymously. Fingerprinting is the technique of identifying a criminal by comparing fingerprints left at the scene of a crime with fingerprints that the police have on file.

5 DNA was first used to solve a crime in 1987, in England. It is considered 99% accurate.

Chapter **8** LECTURE QUIZ ANSWERS

1 The United States is the only Western industrialized country to use the death penalty. In 1972, the U.S. Supreme Court ruled that capital punishment was unconstitutional, but reinstated it in 1976.

2 Many states with the most executions are also the states with the highest homicide rates. This indicates that the death penalty does not deter crime.

3 The death penalty is applied in some states, but not others. Poor males and African Americans are more likely to be executed than whites. It would be impossible to execute everyone who committed a horrific crime.

4 The United States is the most violent industrialized nation. It has about 9 murders a year per 100,000 people. This figure is almost ten times higher than in France, and twenty times almost twenty times higher than in Japan. Fear of violence might explain support for the death penalty.

5 Laws are made to elevate us, to make us stronger, and to let us overcome our emotional response to crime. The legal system is supposed to help us become better than we are.

Chapter 9 LECTURE QUIZ ANSWERS

1 Traditionally, people looked in newspapers or at TV ads to find jobs. Then they made phone calls to prospective employers, sent them a résumé with a cover letter, and waited for a response.

2 It is now possible to research jobs online over a large geographical area. You can send your résumé or job application by e-mail. This makes the process more efficient and more open to people of different socioeconomic backgrounds.

3 Job applicants must still be able to express themselves well and interact with colleagues and clients.

4 In the past, people wrote on paper and stored information in paper calendars, rolodexes, and file cabinets. Today people need to know how to write letters on the computer, create PowerPoint presentations, and organize data in a spreadsheet. Advanced computer users should know how to use databases.

5 You can e-mail your friends and make simple posters with PowerPoint. You can practice storing telephone numbers on premade databases. If you play with the computer in your free time, you will become familiar with its operating system. The Internet also has free tutorials.

Chapter 10 LECTURE QUIZ ANSWERS

1 The world's population is increasing and there is a trend toward mass urbanization that is unprecedented worldwide.

2 One reason for the move to an urban environment is economic. People can make more money in cities, in areas such as information technology and manufacturing and in service areas such as tourism and financing. A second reason has to do with quality of life. Cities often offer better educational opportunities, transportation networks, and entertainment.

3 Cities are getting bigger. Today, there are megacities that have more than 10 million people. Cities are also getting taller. Cities have skyscrapers and tall apartment buildings that hold many more people than small buildings would. Finally, cities are developing urban sprawl, which means that they are spreading out. Some cities, for example the Japanese cities Osaka, Kobe, and Kyoto, are getting linked together because of urban sprawl

4 The Sector Model and the Multiple Nuclei Model show that cities are spreading in an uncontrolled way. In these two models the business district is close to all the other districts. In the Concentric Zone Model the Central Business District is only close to the Wholesale/Light Manufacturing District, and it is far away from the High-Class Residential District.

5 Cities often break up into smaller communities because people from similar backgrounds want to live together. One example is that of migrants to the cities who want to live near people from their own cultural background. Another example is that of people who come to a city from a smaller community and want to live near their friends or family members who are already settled in the city.

Notes